PENGUIN BOOKS — GREAT IDEAS

The Inner Life

City and Islington College

SFC03009

Thomas à Kempis

1380–1471

SFC03009

Thomas à Kempis

The Inner Life

TRANSLATED BY LEO SHERLEY-PRICE

PENGUIN BOOKS — GREAT IDEAS

CITY AND ISLINGTON
SIXTH FORM COLLEGE
283 - 309 GOSWELL ROAD
LONDON
EC1
TEL 020 7520 0652

PENGUIN BOOKS

Published by the Penguin Group
Penguin Books Ltd, 80 Strand, London WC2R ORL, England
Penguin Group (USA) Inc., 375 Hudson Street, New York, New York 10014, USA
Penguin Books Australia Ltd, 250 Camberwell Road,
Camberwell, Victoria 3124, Australia
Penguin Books Canada Ltd, 10 Alcorn Avenue, Toronto, Ontario, Canada M4V 3B2
Penguin Books India (P) Ltd, 11 Community Centre,
Panchsheel Park, New Delhi – 110 017, India
Penguin Group (NZ), Cnr Airborne and Rosedale Roads,
Albany, Auckland 1310, New Zealand
Penguin Books (South Africa) (Pty) Ltd, 24 Sturdee Avenue,
Rosebank 2196, South Africa

Penguin Books Ltd, Registered Offices: 80 Strand, London WC2R ORL, England

www.penguin.com

This translation first published in *The Imitation of Christ* in Penguin Classics 1952
This extract first published in Penguin Books 2004

8

Translation copyright 1952 by Leo Sherley-Price
All rights reserved

Taken from the Penguin Classics edition of *The Imitation of Christ*,
translated and introduced by Leo Sherley-Price

Set in Monotype Dante
Typeset by Rowland Phototypesetting Ltd, Bury St Edmunds, Suffolk
Printed in England by Clays Ltd, St Ives plc

Except in the United States of America, this book is sold subject
to the condition that it shall not, by way of trade or otherwise, be lent,
re-sold, hired out, or otherwise circulated without the publisher's
prior consent in any form of binding or cover other than that in
which it is published and without a similar condition including this
condition being imposed on the subsequent purchaser

Contents

BOOK ONE

Counsels on the Spiritual Life

CHAPTER I
On the Imitation of Christ

'He who follows Me shall not walk in darkness,' says Our Lord.

In these words Christ counsels us to follow His life and way if we desire true enlightenment and freedom from all blindness of heart. Let the life of Jesus Christ, then, be our first consideration.

The teaching of Jesus far transcends all the teachings of the Saints, and whosoever has His spirit will discover concealed in it heavenly manna. But many people, although they often hear the Gospel, feel little desire to follow it, because they lack the spirit of Christ. Whoever desires to understand and take delight in the words of Christ must strive to conform his whole life to Him.

Of what use is it to discourse learnedly on the Trinity, if you lack humility and therefore displease the Trinity? Lofty words do not make a man just or holy; but a good life makes him dear to God. I would far rather feel contrition than be able to define it. If you knew the whole Bible by heart, and all the teachings of the philosophers, how would this help you without the grace and love of God? 'Vanity of vanities, and all is vanity,' except to love God and serve Him alone. And this is supreme wisdom – to despise the world, and draw daily nearer the kingdom of heaven.

It is vanity to solicit honours, or to raise oneself to high station. It is vanity to be a slave to bodily desires, and to crave for things which bring certain retribution. It is vanity to wish for long life, if you care little for a good life. It is vanity to give thought only to this present life, and to care nothing for the life to come. It is vanity to love things that so swiftly pass away, and not to hasten onwards to that place where everlasting joy abides.

Keep constantly in mind the saying, 'The eye is not satisfied with seeing, nor the ear filled with hearing.' Strive to withdraw your heart from the love of visible things, and direct your affections to things invisible. For those who follow only their natural inclinations defile their conscience, and lose the grace of God.

CHAPTER 2
On Personal Humility

Everyone naturally desires knowledge, but of what use is knowledge itself without the fear of God? A humble countryman who serves God is more pleasing to Him than a conceited intellectual who knows the course of the stars, but neglects his own soul. A man who truly knows himself realizes his own worthlessness, and takes no pleasure in the praises of men. Did I possess all knowledge in the world, but had no love, how would this help me before God, who will judge me by my deeds?

Restrain an inordinate desire for knowledge, in which is found much anxiety and deception. Learned men always wish to appear so, and desire recognition of their wisdom. But there are many matters, knowledge of which brings little or no advantage to the soul. Indeed, a man is unwise if he occupies himself with any things save those that further his salvation. A spate of words does nothing to satisfy the soul, but a good life refreshes the mind, and a clean conscience brings great confidence in God.

The more complete and excellent your knowledge, the more severe will be God's judgement on you, unless your life be the more holy. Therefore, do not be conceited of any skill or knowledge you may possess, but respect the knowledge that is entrusted to you. If it seems to you that you know a great deal and have wide experience in many fields, yet remember that there are many matters of which you are ignorant. So do not be conceited, but confess your ignorance. Why do you wish to esteem yourself above others, when there are many who are wiser and more perfect in the Law of God? If you desire to know or learn anything to your advantage, then take delight in being unknown and unregarded.

A true understanding and humble estimate of oneself is the highest and most valuable of all lessons. To take no account of oneself, but always to think well and highly of others is the highest wisdom and perfection. Should you see another person openly doing evil, or carrying out a wicked purpose, do not on that account consider yourself better than him, for you cannot tell how long you will remain in a state of grace. We are all frail; consider none more frail than yourself.

CHAPTER 3
On the Teaching of Truth

Happy the man who is instructed by Truth itself, not by signs and passing words, but as It is in itself. Our own conjectures and observations often mislead us, and we discover little. Of what value are lengthy controversies on deep and obscure matters, when it is not by our knowledge of such things that we shall at length be judged? It is supreme folly to neglect things that are useful and vital, and deliberately turn to curious and harmful things. Truly, 'we have eyes and see not': for what concern to us are such things as *genera* and *species*?

Those to whom the Eternal Word speaks are delivered from uncertainty. From one Word proceed all things, and all things tell of Him; it is He, the Author of all things, who speaks to us. Without Him no one can understand or judge aright. But the man to whom all things are one, who refers everything to One, and who sees everything as in One, is enabled to remain steadfast in heart, and abide at peace with God.

O God, living Truth, unite me to Yourself in everlasting love! Often I am wearied by all I read and hear. In You alone is all that I desire and long for. Therefore let all teachers keep silence, and let all creation be still before You; do You, O Lord, speak alone.

The more closely a man is united to You in pure simplicity, the more varied and profound the matters which he understands without effort, for he receives light and understanding from heaven. A pure, simple, and stable man, however busy and occupied, does not become distracted thereby, for he does all things to the glory of God, and strives to preserve himself free from all self-seeking. And what harms and hinders you more than the undisciplined passions of your own heart? A good and devout man firstly sets in order in his mind whatever tasks he has in hand, and never allows them to lead him into occasions of sin, but humbly subjects them to the dictates of a sound judgement. Who has a fiercer struggle than he who strives to conquer himself? Yet this must be our chief concern – to conquer self, and by daily growing stronger than self, to advance in holiness.

All perfection in this life is accompanied by a measure of imperfection, and all our knowledge contains an element of obscurity. A humble knowledge of oneself is a surer road to God than a deep searching of the sciences. Yet learning itself is not to be blamed, nor is the simple knowledge of anything whatsoever to be despised, for true learning is good in itself and ordained by God; but a good conscience and a holy life are always to be preferred. But because many are more eager to acquire much learning than to live well, they often go astray, and bear little or no fruit. If only such people were as diligent in the uprooting of vices and the planting of virtues as they are in the debating of problems, there would not be so many evils and scandals among the people, nor such laxity in communities. At the Day of Judgement, we shall not be asked what we have read, but what we have done; not how eloquently we have spoken, but how holily we have lived. Tell me, where are now all those Masters and Doctors whom you knew so well in their lifetime in the full flower of their learning? Other men now sit in their seats, and they are hardly ever called to mind. In their lifetime they seemed of great account, but now no one speaks of them.

Oh, how swiftly the glory of the world passes away! If only the lives of these men had been as admirable as their learning, their study and reading would have been to good purpose! But how many in this world care little for the service of God, and perish in their vain learning. Because they choose to be great rather than humble, they perish in their own conceit. He is truly great, who is great in the love of God. He is truly great, who is humble in mind, and regards earth's highest honours as nothing. He is truly wise who counts all earthly things as dung, in order that he may win Christ. And he is truly learned, who renounces his own will for the will of God.

CHAPTER 4
On Prudence in Action

We should not believe every word and suggestion, but should carefully and unhurriedly consider all things in accordance with the will of God. For such is the weakness of human nature, alas, that evil is often more readily believed and spoken of another than good. But perfect men do not easily believe every tale that is told them, for they know that man's nature is prone to evil, and his words to deception.

It is wise not to be over hasty in action, nor to cling stubbornly to our own opinions. It is wise also not to believe all that we hear, nor to hasten to report to others what we hear or believe. Take counsel of a wise and conscientious man, and seek to be guided by one who is better than yourself, rather than to follow your own opinions. A good life makes a man wise towards God, and gives him experience in many things. The more humble and obedient to God a man is, the more wise and at peace he will be in all that he does.

CHAPTER 5
On Reading the Holy Scriptures

In the holy Scriptures, truth is to be looked for rather than fair phrases. All sacred scriptures should be read in the spirit in which they were written. In them, therefore, we should seek food for our souls rather than subtleties of speech, and we should as readily read simple and devout books as those that are lofty and profound. Do not be influenced by the importance of the writer, and whether his learning be great or small, but let the love of pure truth draw you to read. Do not inquire, 'Who said this?' but pay attention to what is said.

Men pass away, but the word of the Lord endures for ever.

God speaks to us in different ways, and is no respecter

of persons. But curiosity often hinders us in the reading of the Scriptures, for we try to examine and dispute over matters that we should pass over and accept in simplicity. If you desire to profit, read with humility, simplicity, and faith, and have no concern to appear learned. Ask questions freely, and listen in silence to the words of the Saints; hear with patience the parables of the fathers, for they are not told without good cause.

CHAPTER 6
On Control of the Desires

Whenever a man desires anything inordinately, at once he becomes restless. A proud and avaricious man is never at rest; but a poor and humble man enjoys the riches of peace. A man who is not yet perfectly dead to self is easily tempted, and is overcome even in small and trifling things. And he who is weak in spirit, and still a prey to the senses and bodily passions, can only with great difficulty free himself from worldly lusts. Therefore he is sad when he does so withdraw himself, and is quickly angered when anyone opposes him. Yet, if he obtains what he desires, his conscience is at once stricken by remorse, because he has yielded to his passion, which in no way helps him in his search for peace. True peace of heart can be found only by resisting the passions, not by yielding to them. There is no peace in the heart of a worldly man, who is entirely given to outward affairs; but only in a fervent, spiritual man.

CHAPTER 7
On Avoiding Vain Hope and Conceit

Whoever puts his confidence in men or in any creature is very foolish. Do not be ashamed to be the servant of others for love of Jesus Christ, and to appear poor in this world. Do not trust in yourself, but put your whole confidence in God. Do what you are able, and God will bless your good intention. Do not trust in your own knowledge, nor in the cleverness of any man living, but rather in the grace of God, who aids the humble, and humbles the proud.

Do not boast of your possessions, if you have any, nor of the influence of your friends; but glory in God, who gives all things and desires above all things to give you Himself. Do not be vain about your beauty or strength of body, which a little sickness can mar and disfigure. Take no pleasure in your own ability and cleverness, lest you offend God, who has Himself bestowed on you all your natural gifts.

Do not esteem yourself better than others, lest you appear worse in the eyes of God, who alone knows the heart of man. Do not be proud of your good deeds, for God does not judge as men; and what delights men often displeases God. If you have any good qualities, remember that others have more; and so remain humble. It does you no harm when you esteem all others better than yourself, but it does you great harm when you esteem yourself above others. True peace dwells only in the heart of the humble: but the heart of the proud is ever full of pride and jealousy.

[. . .]

CHAPTER 10
On Avoiding Talkativeness

Avoid public gatherings as much as possible, for the discussion of worldly affairs becomes a great hindrance, even though it be with the best of intentions, for we are quickly corrupted and ensnared by vanity. Often I wish I had remained silent, and had not been among men. But why is it that we are so ready to chatter and gossip with each other, when we so seldom return to silence without some injury to our conscience? The reason why we are so fond of talking with each other is that we think to find consolation in this manner, and to refresh a heart wearied with many cares. And we prefer to speak and think of those things which we like and desire, or of those which we dislike. Alas, however, all this is often to no purpose, for this outward consolation is no small obstacle to inner and divine consolation.

We must watch and pray, that our time may not be spent fruitlessly. When it is right and proper to speak, speak to edify. Evil habits and neglect of spiritual progress are the main cause of our failure to guard the tongue. But devout conversation on spiritual matters greatly furthers our spiritual progress, especially with those who are heart and soul with us in the service of God.

CHAPTER II
On Peace, and Spiritual Progress

We could enjoy much peace if we did not busy ourselves with what other people say and do, for this is no concern of ours. How can anyone remain long at peace who meddles in other people's affairs; who seeks occasion to gad about, and who makes little or no attempt at recollection? Blessed are the single-hearted, for they shall enjoy much peace.

How were some of the Saints so perfect and contemplative? It is because they strove with all their might to mortify in themselves all worldly desires, and could thus cling to God in their inmost heart, and offer themselves freely and wholly to Him. But we are held too firmly by our passions, and are too much concerned with the passing affairs of the world. We seldom completely master a single fault, and have little zeal for our daily progress; therefore we remain spiritually cold or tepid.

If only we were completely dead to self, and free from inner conflict, we could savour spiritual things, and win experience of heavenly contemplation. But the greatest, and indeed the whole obstacle to our advance is that we are not free from passions and lusts, nor do we strive to follow the perfect way of the Saints. But when we encounter even a little trouble, we are quickly discouraged, and turn to human comfort.

If we strove to stand firm in the struggle like men of valour, we should not fail to experience the help of our Lord from heaven. For He is ever ready to help all who fight, trusting in His grace; He also affords us occasions to fight that we may conquer. If we rely only on the outward observances of religion, our devotion will rapidly wane. But let us lay the axe to the root, that, being cleansed from our passions, we may possess our souls in peace.

If each year we would root out one fault, we should soon become perfect. But, alas, the opposite is often the case, that we were better and purer in the beginning of our conversion than after many years of our profession. Our zeal and virtue should grow daily; but it is now held to be a fine thing if a man retains even a little of his first fervour. If only we would do a little violence to ourselves at first, we would later be enabled to do everything easily and gladly.

It is hard to give up old habits, and harder still to conquer our own wills. But if you cannot overcome in small and easy things, how will you succeed in greater? Resist your evil inclinations in the beginning, and break off evil habits, lest they gradually involve you in greater difficulties. Oh, if you could only know how great a peace for yourself and how great a joy for your fellows your good endeavour would win, you would have greater care for your spiritual progress.

CHAPTER 12
On the Uses of Adversity

It is good for us to encounter troubles and adversities from time to time, for trouble often compels a man to search his own heart. It reminds him that he is an exile here, and that he can put his trust in nothing in this world. It is good, too, that we sometimes suffer opposition, and that men think ill of us and misjudge us, even when we do and mean well. Such things are an aid to humility, and preserve us from pride and vainglory. For we more readily turn to God as our inward witness, when men despise us and think no good of us.

A man should therefore place such complete trust in God, that he has no need of comfort from men. When a good man is troubled, tempted, or vexed by evil thoughts, he comes more clearly than ever to realize his need of God, without whom he can do nothing good. Then, as he grieves and laments his lot, he turns to prayer amid his misfortunes. He is weary of life, and longs for death to release him, that he may be dissolved, and be with Christ. It is then that he knows with certainty that there can be no complete security nor perfect peace in his life.

CHAPTER 13
On Resisting Temptations

So long as we live in this world, we cannot remain without trial and temptation: as Job says, 'Man's life on earth is a warfare.' We must therefore be on guard against temptations, and watchful in prayer, that the Devil find no means of deceiving us; for he never rests, but prowls around seeking whom he may devour. No one is so perfect and holy that he is never tempted, and we can never be secure from temptation.

Although temptations are so troublesome and grievous, yet they are often profitable to us, for by them we are humbled, cleansed, and instructed. All the Saints endured many trials and temptations, and profited by them; but those who could not resist temptations became reprobate, and fell away. There is no Order so holy, nor place so secluded, where there are no troubles and temptations.

No man can be entirely free from temptation so long as he lives; for the source of temptation lies within our own nature, since we are born with an inclination towards evil. When one temptation or trial draws to a close, another takes its place; and we shall always have something to fight, for man has lost the blessing of original happiness. Many try to escape temptations, only to encounter them more fiercely, for no one can win victory by flight alone; it is only by patience and true humility that we can grow stronger than all our foes.

The man who only avoids the outward occasions of evil, but fails to uproot it in himself, will gain little advantage. Indeed, temptations will return upon him the sooner, and he will find himself in a worse state than before. Little by little and by patient endurance you will overcome them by God's help, better than by your own violence and importunity. Seek regular advice in temptation, and never deal harshly with those who are tempted, but give them such encouragement as you would value yourself.

The beginning of all evil temptation is an unstable mind and lack of trust in God. Just as a ship without a helm is driven to and fro by the waves, so a careless man, who abandons his proper course, is tempted in countless ways. Fire tempers steel, and temptation the just man. We often do not know what we can bear, but temptation reveals our true nature. We need especially to be on our guard at the very onset of temptation, for then the Enemy may be more easily overcome, if he is not allowed to enter the gates of the mind: he must be repulsed at the threshold, as soon as he knocks. Thus the poet Ovid writes, 'Resist at the beginning; the remedy may come too late.' For first there comes into the mind an evil thought: next, a vivid picture: then delight, and urge to evil, and finally consent. In this way the Enemy gradually gains complete mastery, when he is not resisted at first. And the longer a slothful man delays resistance, the weaker he becomes, and the stronger his enemy grows against him.

Some people undergo their heaviest temptations at the beginning of their conversion; some towards the end of their course; others are greatly troubled all their lives; while there are some whose temptations are but light. This is in accordance with the wisdom and justice of God's ordinance, who weighs the condition and merits of every man, and disposes all things for the salvation of those whom He chooses.

We must not despair, therefore, when we are tempted, but earnestly pray God to grant us his help in every need. For, as Saint Paul says, 'With the temptation, God will provide a way to overcome it, that we may be able to bear it.' So, let us humble ourselves under the hand of God in every trial and trouble, for He will save and raise up the humble in spirit. In all these trials, our progress is tested; in them great merit may be secured, and our virtue become evident. It is no great matter if we are devout and fervent when we have no troubles; but if we show patience in adversity, we can make great progress in virtue. Some are spared severe temptations, but are overcome in the lesser ones of every day, in order that they may be humble, and learn not to trust in themselves, but to recognize their frailty.

CHAPTER 14
On Avoiding Rash Judgements

Judge yourself, and beware of passing judgement on others. In judging others, we expend our energy to no purpose; we are often mistaken, and easily sin. But if we judge ourselves, our labour is always to our profit. Our judgement is frequently influenced by our personal feelings, and it is very easy to fail in right judgement when we are inspired by private motives. Were God Himself the sole and constant object of our desire, we should not be so easily distressed when our opinions are contradicted.

Very often some inner impulse or outward circumstance draws us to follow it, while many people are always acting in their own interest, although they are not conscious of it. Such appear to enjoy complete tranquillity of mind so long as events accord with their wishes, but at once become distressed and disconsolate when things fall out otherwise. Similarly, differences of opinions and beliefs only too often give rise to quarrels among friends and neighbours, and even between religious and devout people.

Old habits are hard to break, and no one is easily weaned from his own opinions; but if you rely on your own reasoning and ability rather than on the virtue of submission to Jesus Christ, you will but seldom and slowly attain wisdom. For God wills that we become perfectly obedient to Himself, and that we transcend mere reason on the wings of a burning love for Him.

CHAPTER 15

On Deeds Inspired by Love

No motive, even that of affection for anyone, can justify the doing of evil. But to help someone in need, a good work may sometimes be left, or a better undertaken in its place. For in so doing, the good work is not lost, but changed for what is better. Without love, the outward work is of no value; but whatever is done out of love, be it never so little, is wholly fruitful. For God regards the greatness of the love that prompts a man, rather than the greatness of his achievement.

Whoever loves much, does much. Whoever does a thing well, does much. And he does well, who serves the community before his own interests. Often an apparently loving action really springs from worldly motives; for natural inclination, self-will, hope of reward, and our own self-interest will seldom be entirely absent.

Whoever is moved by true and perfect love is never self-seeking, but desires only that God's glory may be served in all things. He envies none, for he seeks no pleasure for himself, nor does he act for self-gratification, but desires above all good things to merit the blessing of God. All good he ascribes not to men, but to God, from whom all things proceed as from their source, and in whom all the Saints enjoy perfection and peace. Oh, if only a man had a spark of true love in his heart, he would know for certain that all earthly things are full of vanity.

CHAPTER 16
On Bearing with the Faults of Others

Whatever a man is unable to correct in himself or in others, he should bear patiently until God ordains otherwise. Consider, it is perhaps better thus, for the testing of our patience, without which our merits are of little worth. Whenever such obstacles confront you, pray to God that He may grant you His help, and give you grace to endure them in good heart.

If anyone who has been once or twice warned remains obdurate, do not argue with him, but commit all things to God, that His will may be done, and His Name hallowed in all His servants; for He knows well how to bring good out of evil. Strive to be patient; bear with the faults and frailties of others, for you, too, have many faults which others have to bear. If you cannot mould yourself as you would wish, how can you expect other people to be entirely to your liking? For we require other people to be perfect, but do not correct our own faults.

We wish to see others severely reprimanded; yet we are unwilling to be corrected ourselves. We wish to restrict the liberty of others, but are not willing to be denied anything ourselves. We wish others to be bound by rules, yet we will not let ourselves be bound. It is amply evident, therefore, that we seldom consider our neighbour in the same light as ourselves. Yet, if all men were perfect, what should we have to bear with in others for Christ's sake?

Now, God has thus ordered things that we may learn to bear one another's burdens; for there is no man without his faults, none without his burden. None is sufficient in himself; none is wise in himself; therefore we must support one another, comfort, help, teach, and advise one another. Times of trouble best discover the true worth of a man; they do not weaken him, but show his true nature.

[. . .]

CHAPTER 23
A Meditation on Death

Very soon the end of your life will be at hand: consider, therefore, the state of your soul. Today a man is here; tomorrow he is gone. And when he is out of sight, he is soon out of mind. Oh, how dull and hard is the heart of man, which thinks only of the present, and does not provide against the future! You should order your every deed and thought, as though today were the day of your death. Had you a good conscience, death would hold no terrors for you; even so, it were better to avoid sin than to escape death. If you are not ready to die today, will tomorrow find you better prepared? Tomorrow is uncertain; and how can you be sure of tomorrow?

Of what use is a long life, if we amend so little? Alas, a long life often adds to our sins rather than to our virtue!

Would to God that we might spend a single day really well! Many recount the years since their conversion, but their lives show little sign of improvement. If it is dreadful to die, it is perhaps more dangerous to live long. Blessed is the man who keeps the hour of his death always in mind, and daily prepares himself to die. If you have ever seen anyone die, remember that you, too, must travel the same road.

Each morning remember that you may not live until evening; and in the evening, do not presume to promise yourself another day. Be ready at all times, and so live that death may never find you unprepared. Many die suddenly and unexpectedly; for at an hour that we do not know the Son of Man will come. When your last hour strikes, you will begin to think very differently of your past life, and grieve deeply that you have been so careless and remiss.

Happy and wise is he who endeavours to be during his life as he wishes to be found at his death. For these things will afford us sure hope of a happy death; perfect contempt of the world; fervent desire to grow in holiness; love of discipline; the practice of penance; ready obedience; self-denial; the bearing of every trial for the love of Christ. While you enjoy health, you can do much good; but when sickness comes, little can be done. Few are made better by sickness, and those who make frequent pilgrimages seldom acquire holiness by so doing.

Do not rely on friends and neighbours, and do not delay the salvation of your soul to some future date, for men will forget you sooner than you think. It is better to make timely provision and to acquire merit in this life, than to depend on the help of others. And if you have no care for your own soul, who will have care for you in time to come? The present time is most precious; now is the accepted time, now is the day of salvation. It is sad that you do not employ your time better, when you may win eternal life hereafter. The time will come when you will long for one day or one hour in which to amend; and who knows whether it will be granted?

Dear soul, from what peril and fear you could free yourself, if you lived in holy fear, mindful of your death. Apply yourself so to live now, that at the hour of death, you may be glad and unafraid. Learn now to die to the world, that you may begin to live with Christ. Learn now to despise all earthly things, that you may go freely to Christ. Discipline your body now by penance, that you may enjoy a sure hope of salvation.

Foolish man, how can you promise yourself a long life, when you are not certain of a single day? How many have deceived themselves in this way, and been snatched unexpectedly from life! You have often heard how this man was slain by the sword; another drowned; how another fell from a high place and broke his neck; how another died at table; how another met his end in play. One perishes by fire, another by the sword, another from disease, another at the hands of robbers. Death is the end of all men; and the life of man passes away suddenly as a shadow.

Who will remember you when you are dead? Who will pray for you? Act now, dear soul; do all you can; for you know neither the hour of your death, nor your state after death. While you have time, gather the riches of everlasting life. Think only of your salvation, and care only for the things of God. Make friends now, by honouring the Saints of God and by following their example, that when this life is over, they may welcome you to your eternal home.

Keep yourself a stranger and pilgrim upon earth, to whom the affairs of this world are of no concern. Keep your heart free and lifted up to God, for here you have no abiding city. Daily direct your prayers and longings to Heaven, that at your death your soul may merit to pass joyfully into the presence of God.

[. . .]

BOOK TWO

Counsels on the Inner Life

CHAPTER I
On the Inner Life

'The Kingdom of God is within you,' says Our Lord. Turn to the Lord with all your heart, forsake this sorry world, and your soul shall find rest. Learn to turn from worldly things, and give yourself to spiritual things, and you will see the Kingdom of God come within you. For the Kingdom is peace and joy in the Holy Spirit; these are not granted to the wicked. Christ will come to you, and impart his consolations to you, if you prepare a worthy dwelling for Him in your heart. All true glory and beauty is within, and there He delights to dwell. He often visits the spiritual man, and holds sweet discourse with him, granting him refreshing grace, great peace, and friendship exceeding all expectation.

Come then, faithful soul; prepare your heart for your Divine Spouse, that He may deign to come to you and dwell with you. For He says, 'If any man love Me, he will keep My word; and We will come and make Our abode with him.' Therefore welcome Christ, and deny entrance to all others. When you possess Christ, you are amply rich, and He will satisfy you. He will dispose and

23

provide for you faithfully in everything, so that you need not rely on man. For men soon change and fail you; but Christ abides for ever, and stands firmly by you to the end.

Never place your whole trust and reliance in weak and mortal man, however helpful and dear to you he may be; nor should you grieve overmuch if sometimes he opposes and contradicts you. Those who take your part today may tomorrow oppose you; for men are as changeable as the weather. Put your whole trust in God; direct your worship and love to Him alone. He will defend you, and will dispose all things for the best. Here you have no abiding city, and wherever you may be, you are a stranger and pilgrim; you will never enjoy peace until you become inwardly united to Christ.

What do you seek here, since this world is not your resting place? Your true home is in Heaven; therefore remember that all the things of this world are transitory. All things are passing, and yourself with them. See that you do not cling to them, lest you become entangled and perish with them. Let all your thoughts be with the Most High, and direct your humble prayers unceasingly to Christ. If you cannot contemplate high and heavenly things, take refuge in the Passion of Christ, and love to dwell within His Sacred Wounds. For if you devoutly seek the Wounds of Jesus and the precious marks of His Passion, you will find great strength in all troubles. And if men despise you, you will care little, having small regard for the words of your detractors.

Christ Himself was despised by men, and in His direst need was abandoned by his friends and acquaintances to the insults of His enemies. Christ was willing to suffer and to be despised; and do you presume to complain? Christ had enemies and slanderers; and do you expect all men to be your friends and benefactors? How will your patience be crowned, if you are not willing to endure hardship? Suffer with Christ, and for Christ, if you wish to reign with Christ.

Had you but once entered perfectly into the Heart of Jesus, and tasted something of His burning love, you would care nothing for your own gain or loss; for the love of Jesus causes a man to regard himself very humbly. The true, inward lover of Jesus and the Truth, who is free from inordinate desires, can turn freely to God, rise above self, and joyfully rest in God.

He who knows all things at their true worth, and not as they are said or reputed to be, is truly wise, for his knowledge comes from God, and not from man. He who walks by an inner light, and is not unduly influenced by outward things, needs no special time or place for his prayers. For the man of inner life easily recollects himself, since he is never wholly immersed in outward affairs. Therefore his outward occupations and needful tasks do not distract him, and he adjusts himself to things as they come. The man whose inner life is well-ordered and disposed is not troubled by the strange and perverse ways of others; for a man is hindered and distracted by such things only so far as he allows himself to be concerned by them.

If your inner life were rightly ordered and your heart pure, all things would turn to your good and advantage. As it is, you are often displeased and disturbed, because you are not yet completely dead to self, nor detached from all worldly things. Nothing defiles and ensnares the heart of man more than a selfish love of creatures. If you renounce all outward consolation, you will be able to contemplate heavenly things, and often experience great joy of heart.

CHAPTER 2
On Humble Submission to God

Do not be concerned overmuch who is with you or against you, but work and plan that God may be with you in all that you do. Keep a clean conscience, and God will mightily defend you; for whoever enjoys the protection of God cannot be harmed by the malice of man. If you learn to suffer in silence, you may be sure of receiving God's help. He knows the time and the way to deliver you; so trust yourself entirely to His care. God is strong to help you, and to free you from all confusion. It is often good for us that others know and expose our faults, for so may we be kept humble.

When a man humbly admits his faults, he soon appeases his fellows, and is reconciled to those whom he had offended. God protects and delivers a humble man; He loves and comforts him. To the humble He leans down and bestows great success, raising him from abasement to honour. To him He reveals His secrets, and lovingly calls and draws him to Himself. Even in the midst of trouble, the humble man remains wholly at peace, for he trusts in God, and not in the world. Do not consider yourself to have made any spiritual progress, unless you account yourself the least of all men.

CHAPTER 3
On the Good and Peaceful Man

Firstly, be peaceful yourself, and you will be able to bring peace to others. A man of peace does more good than a very learned man. A passionate man turns even good into evil, and readily listens to evil; but a good and peaceable man turns all things to good. He who is truly at peace thinks evil of no one; but he who is discontented and restless is tormented by suspicions beyond number. He has no peace in himself, nor will he allow others any peace. He often says what he ought not to say, and leaves undone what he should have done. He takes note how other people carry out their duties, but neglects his own. Therefore, before all else, attend diligently to your own affairs; then you may properly be concerned for your neighbour also.

You readily excuse and explain your own doings, but you will not accept the explanations of others. It would be more just to accuse yourself, and to excuse your fellows. If you wish others to bear with you, you must bear with them. See how far you still are from true charity and humility, which feels no anger nor indignation towards any save itself. It is no great matter to associate with the good and gentle, for this is naturally pleasant to everyone. All men are glad to live at peace, and prefer those who are of their own way of thinking.

But to be able to live at peace among hard, obstinate, and undisciplined people and those who oppose us, is a great grace, and a most commendable and manly achievement.

There are some who remain at peace with themselves and also with others. And some neither have peace in themselves nor allow others to have peace. Such people are a trouble to others, and an even greater trouble to themselves. And there are some who are at peace with themselves, and who try to guide others into peace. But all our peace in this present life should depend on humble forbearance rather than on absence of adversity. He who knows the secret of endurance will enjoy the greatest peace. Such a one is conqueror of self, master of the world, a friend of Christ, and an heir of Heaven.

CHAPTER 4

On Purity of Mind and Simplicity of Purpose

There are two wings that raise a man above earthly things – simplicity and purity. Simplicity must inspire his purpose, and purity his affection. Simplicity reaches out after God; purity discovers and enjoys Him. No good deed will prove an obstacle to you if you are inwardly free from uncontrolled desires. And if you are free from uncontrolled desires, and seek nothing but the Will of God and the good of your neighbour, you will enjoy this inner freedom. If your heart be right, then every created thing will become for you a mirror of life and a book of holy teaching. For there is nothing created so small and mean that it does not reflect the goodness of God.

Were you inwardly good and pure, you would see and understand all things clearly and without difficulty. A pure heart penetrates both heaven and hell. As each man is in himself, so does he judge outward things. If there is any joy to be had in this world, the pure in heart most surely possess it; and if there is trouble and distress anywhere, the evil conscience most readily experiences it. Just as iron, when plunged into fire, loses its rust and becomes bright and glowing, so the man who turns himself wholly to God loses his sloth and becomes transformed into a new creature.

When a man begins to grow dull and lukewarm in spirit, even the smallest labour distresses him, and he eagerly welcomes any worldly comfort. But when he begins to overcome self and advance manfully in God's way, then he regards as nothing those labours which he previously found so burdensome.

CHAPTER 5
On Knowing Ourselves

We may not trust overmuch in ourselves, for we often lack grace and understanding. There is little light in us, and even this we easily lose through carelessness. Moreover, we often do not realize how blind we are. We often do evil, and we do worse in excusing ourselves. Sometimes we are moved by passion, and mistake it for Zeal. We rebuke small faults in others, but overlook greater faults in ourselves. We are too quick to resent and feel what we suffer from others, but fail to consider how much others suffer from us. Whoever considers his own defects fully and honestly will find no reason to judge others harshly.

The spiritual man puts the care of his soul before all else; and whoever diligently attends to his own affairs is ready to keep silence about others. You will never become interior and devout unless you refrain from criticism of others, and pay attention to yourself. If you are wholly intent on God and yourself, you will be little affected by anything outside this. Where are you when you fail to attend to yourself? And when you have occupied yourself in countless affairs, what have you gained, if you have neglected your soul? If you really desire true peace and union with God, attend to yourself, and set aside all else.

Keep yourself free from all worldly entanglement, and you will make good progress; but if you set great value on any worldly things, it will prove a great obstacle. Let nothing be great, pleasant or desirable to you save God alone, and whatever comes of God. Regard as empty comfort all things that derive from creatures. The soul that loves God regards as worthless all things other than God. God alone is eternal and immeasurable, filling all things; He alone is the true comfort of the soul and joy of the heart.

CHAPTER 6
On the Joys of a Good Conscience

The glory of a good man is the witness of a good conscience. Preserve a quiet conscience, and you will always have joy. A quiet conscience can endure much, and remains joyful in all trouble, but an evil conscience is always fearful and uneasy. You may rest easy if your heart does not reproach you, and you are happy only when you have done right. The wicked never know true happiness, nor do they enjoy inward peace, for 'There is no peace for the wicked,' says the Lord. And although they say, 'We are at peace; no evil happens to us, and no one will dare to harm us,' yet God's anger will rise suddenly, all their works will be brought to nothing, and their plans perish.

To glory in suffering is not hard for one who truly loves God, for so to glory is to glory in the Cross of our Lord. Short-lived is the glory that is granted and received by men, and sorrow is ever its companion. The glory of good men is in their own conscience, not in the tongues of men. For the joy of the Saints is from God and in God, and their joy is in the truth. Whoever desires true and lasting glory cares nothing for worldly glory. And whoever craves worldly glory, or who does not at heart despise it, shows himself to have little love for the glory of heaven. Great tranquillity of heart is his who cares for neither praise nor blame.

The man who has a clean conscience rests easily content, and is at peace. You are none the holier for being praised, and none the worse for being blamed. You remain what you are, nor can you be accounted greater than you are in the sight of God. If you take heed to what you are inwardly, you will not mind what men say of you; for while man looks on outward appearance, God looks into your heart. Man sees your actions, but God your motives. The sign of a humble soul is always to be doing good, and to think little of oneself. To desire no comfort from creatures is a sign of great purity and inward faith.

When a man seeks no other witness but himself, he shows that he puts his whole trust in God. For, as Saint Paul says, 'Not he who commends himself is approved, but he whom God commends.' To live inwardly to God, and not to be bound by worldly affections, is the proper state of a spiritual man.

CHAPTER 7

On Loving Jesus above all Things

Blessed is he who understands what it is to love Jesus, and to despise himself for Jesus' sake. You must surrender all other love for His love, for Jesus desires to be loved alone, and above all things. The love of creatures is deceptive and unstable; the love of Jesus is faithful and enduring. Whoever clings to any creature will fall with its falling; but he who holds to Jesus shall stand firm for ever. Love Him, therefore, and keep Him as your friend; for when all others desert you, He will not abandon you, nor allow you to perish at the last. Whether you wish it or not, you must in the end be parted from them all.

Hold fast to Jesus, both in life and death, and trust yourself to His faithfulness, for He alone can aid you when all others fail. Your Beloved is of such a nature that He will not share your love with another; He desires your heart for Himself alone, and to reign there as a King on His throne. If you could empty your heart of all creatures, Jesus would delight to dwell with you. Whatever trust you place in men rather than in Jesus is almost wholly wasted. Do not trust or lean on a wind-blown reed, for 'all flesh is as grass, and its glory will fall like the flower of the grass.'

If you look only to men's outward appearance, you will soon be deceived; for if you seek comfort or gain from others, you will often meet with loss. If you seek Jesus in all things, you will surely find Jesus. And if you seek yourself, you will surely find yourself, but only to your ruin. For a man who does not seek Jesus does himself greater hurt than the whole world and all his enemies could ever do him.

[. . .]

CHAPTER 12
On the Royal Road of the Holy Cross

'Deny yourself, take up your cross, and follow Me.' To many this saying of Jesus seems hard. But how much harder will it be to hear that word of doom, 'Depart from

Me, you cursed, into everlasting fire'. For those who now cheerfully hear and obey the word of the Cross will not tremble to hear the sentence of eternal damnation. The sign of the Cross will appear in the heavens, when Our Lord comes as Judge. Then will all the servants of the Cross, who in their lives conformed themselves to the Crucified, stand with confidence before Christ their Judge.

Why, then, do you fear to take up the Cross, which is the road to the Kingdom? In the Cross is salvation; in the Cross is life; in the Cross is protection against our enemies; in the Cross is infusion of heavenly sweetness; in the Cross is strength of mind; in the Cross is joy of spirit; in the Cross is excellence of virtue; in the Cross is perfection of holiness. There is no salvation of soul, nor hope of eternal life, save in the Cross. Take up the Cross, therefore, and follow Jesus, and go forward into eternal life. Christ has gone before you, bearing His Cross; He died for you on the Cross, that you also may bear your cross, and desire to die on the cross with Him. For if you die with Him, you will also live with Him. And if you share His sufferings, you will also share His glory.

See how in the Cross all things consist, and in dying on it all things depend. There is no other way to life and to true inner peace, than the way of the Cross, and of daily self-denial. Go where you will, seek what you will; you will find no higher way above nor safer way below than the road of the Holy Cross. Arrange and order all things to your own ideas and wishes, yet you will still find suffering to endure, whether you will or not; so you will always find the Cross. For you will either endure bodily pain, or suffer anguish of mind and spirit.

At times, God will withdraw from you; at times you will be troubled by your neighbour, and, what is more, you will often be a burden to yourself. Neither can any remedy or comfort bring you relief, but you must bear it as long as God wills. For God desires that you learn to bear trials without comfort, that you may yield yourself wholly to Him, and grow more humble through tribulation. No man feels so deeply in his heart the Passion of Christ as he who has to suffer in like manner. The Cross always stands ready, and everywhere awaits you. You cannot escape it, wherever you flee; for wherever you go, you bear yourself, and always find yourself. Look up or down, without you or within, and everywhere you will find the Cross. And everywhere you must have patience, if you wish to attain inner peace, and win an eternal crown.

If you bear the cross willingly, it will bear you and lead you to your desired goal, where pain shall be no more; but it will not be in this life. If you bear the cross unwillingly, you make it a burden, and load yourself more heavily; but you must needs bear it. If you cast away one cross, you will certainly find another, and perhaps a heavier.

Do you think to escape what no mortal man has been able to escape? Which of the Saints lived without cross or trial? Even our Lord Jesus Christ was never without sorrow and pain, as long as He lived. 'Christ must needs suffer,' said He, 'and rise again from the dead, and so enter into His glory.' Why, then, do you seek any other road than this royal road of the Holy Cross? The whole life of Christ was a cross and martyrdom; and do you look for rest and selfish pleasure?

You are greatly mistaken if you look for anything save to endure trials, for all this mortal life is full of troubles, and everywhere marked with crosses. The further a man advances in the spiritual life, the heavier and more numerous he finds the crosses, for his ever-deepening love of God makes more bitter the sorrows of his earthly exile.

Yet a man who is afflicted in many ways is not without solace and comfort, for he perceives the great benefit to be reaped from the bearing of his cross. For while he bears it with a good will, the whole burden is changed into hope of God's comfort. And the more the body is subdued by affliction, the more is the spirit strengthened by grace within. Sometimes he is so greatly comforted by the desire to suffer adversity for love of conforming to the Cross of Christ, that he would not wish to be without grief and pain; for he knows that the more he can suffer for His sake, the more pleasing he will be to God. This desire does not spring from man's own strength, but from the grace of Christ, which can and does effect such great things in the frail frame of man; so that which nature fears and avoids, he boldly meets and loves through ardour of spirit.

Man is not by nature inclined to carry the cross, to love the cross, to chasten the body, and bring it into subjection; to refuse honours, to submit to insults with goodwill, to despise himself and welcome disparagement; to bear all adversity and loss, and to desire no kind of prosperity in this world. And if you trust in your own strength, you will be unable to achieve any of these things. But if you trust in the Lord, you will be given strength from Heaven, and the world and the flesh will become subject to your will. Neither will you fear your enemy the Devil, if you are armed with faith and signed with the Cross of Christ.

Resolve, then, as a good and faithful servant of Christ, manfully to bear the cross of your Lord, who was crucified for love of you. Prepare yourself to endure many trials and obstacles in this vale of tears; for such will be your lot wherever you are, and you will encounter them wherever you conceal yourself. It must needs be so; nor is there any remedy or means of escape from ills and griefs; you must endure them. Drink lovingly the cup of your Lord, if you wish to be His friend, and to share all with Him. Leave consolations to God, to dispose as He wills. But set yourself to endure trials, regarding them as the greatest of all comforts, 'for the sufferings of this present time are not worthy to be compared with the glory to come', even though you alone were to endure them all.

When you have arrived at that state when trouble seems sweet and acceptable to you for Christ's sake, then all is well with you, for you have found paradise upon earth. But so long as suffering is grievous to you and you seek to escape it, so long will it go ill with you, for the trouble you try to escape will pursue you everywhere.

If you steel yourself – as you must – to suffer and to die, all will go better with you, and you will find peace. For although, like Saint Paul, you were 'caught up into the third heaven', you would not on this account be secured against suffering further adversity. For Jesus says, 'I will show him how great things he must suffer for My

Name.' Therefore, be prepared to suffer, if you wish to love Jesus and serve Him for ever.

Oh, if only you were worthy to suffer for the Name of Jesus! How great and enduring a glory would be yours! How great would be the joy of the Saints of God! How edified your friends would be! For all men commend patience, although few are willing to suffer. It is right that you should suffer a little for the sake of Christ, since many suffer greater things for worldly motives.

Be assured of this, that you must live a dying life. And the more completely a man dies to self, the more he begins to live to God. No man is fit to understand heavenly things, unless he is resigned to bear hardships for Christ's sake. Nothing is more acceptable to God, and nothing more salutary for yourself, than to suffer gladly for Christ's sake. And if it lies in your choice, you should choose rather to suffer hardships for Christ's sake, than to be refreshed by many consolations; for thus you will more closely resemble Christ and all His Saints. For our merit and spiritual progress does not consist in enjoying such sweetness and consolation, but rather in the bearing of great burdens and troubles.

Had there been a better way, more profitable to the salvation of mankind than suffering, then Christ would have revealed it in His word and life. But He clearly urges both His own disciples and all who wish to follow Him to carry the cross, saying, 'If any will come after Me, let him deny himself, and take up his cross and follow Me.' Therefore, when we have read and studied all things, let this be our final resolve: 'that through much tribulation we must enter the Kingdom of God.'

BOOK THREE
On Inward Consolation

CHAPTER I
How Christ Speaks Inwardly to the Soul

'I will hear what the Lord God speaks within me.' Blessed is the soul that hears the Lord speaking within it, and receives comfort from His Word. Blessed are the ears that hear the still, small voice of God, and disregard the whispers of the world. Blessed are the ears that listen to Truth teaching inwardly, and not to the voices of the world. Blessed are the eyes that are closed to outward things, but are open to inward things. Blessed are those who enter deeply into inner things, and daily prepare themselves to receive the secrets of heaven. Blessed are those who strive to devote themselves wholly to God, and free themselves from all the entanglements of the world. Consider these things, O my soul, and shut fast the doors against the desires of the senses, that you may hear what the Lord your God speaks within you.

Your Beloved says: 'I am your Salvation, your Peace, and your Life; keep close to Me, and you shall find peace.' Set aside the things of time, and seek those of eternity; for what are the things of time but deceits? And how can any creature help you, if your Creator abandon you? Set aside, therefore, all else, and make yourself acceptable to your Creator, and be faithful to Him, that you may lay hold on true blessedness.

CHAPTER 2
How Truth Instructs us in Silence

THE DISCIPLE. 'Speak, Lord, for Your servant listens.' 'I am Your servant; grant me understanding, that I may know Your testimonies.' 'Incline my heart to the words of Your mouth; let Your speech descend on me like the dew.' The people of Israel of old time said to Moses, 'Speak with us, and we will hear: let not God speak with us, lest we die.' But I do not pray thus, O Lord; but with the Prophet Samuel, I humbly and earnestly beg, 'Speak, Lord, for your servant listens.' Let not Moses or any of the Prophets speak to me, but rather do You speak, O Lord God, who inspire and enlighten the Prophets. You alone can perfectly instruct me without their aid, but without You they can do nothing.

The Prophets can preach the word, but they cannot bestow the Spirit. They speak most eloquently, but if You are silent, they cannot fire the heart. They instruct in the letter, but You open the understanding. They set forth the mysteries, but You reveal the meaning of all secrets. They teach your commandments, but You help us to observe them. They point the way, but You grant us strength to follow it. Their action is external; You instruct and enlighten the heart. They water the seed; You make it fruitful. They proclaim the words, but You impart understanding to the mind.

Therefore, let not Moses speak to me, but You, O Lord my God, the Everlasting Truth, lest I die and bear no fruit if I am but warned in word, and not kindled at heart; lest it turn to my condemnation, if I hear Your word, but do not obey it; know it, but do not love it; believe it, but do not keep it. Therefore, speak, Lord, for Your servant is listening. 'You have the words of eternal life.' Speak to me, Lord, and comfort my soul: order my life to Your praise, glory, and eternal honour.

CHAPTER 3
On Humble Attention to God's Word

CHRIST. My son, hear My words. They are of surpassing sweetness, and excel all the learning of the philosophers and wise men of this world. My words are spirit and life, not to be weighed by man's understanding. They are not to be quoted for vain pleasure, but are to be heard in silence, and received with all humility and love.

THE DISCIPLE. Blessed is the man whom you instruct, O Lord, and teach him out of Your Law. You refresh him in evil days, and he will not be desolate on the earth.

CHRIST. I have taught the Prophets from the beginning of the world, and I do not cease to speak to all men today; but many are hardened, and deaf to My voice.

Many listen more willingly to the world than to God, and would rather follow the desires of the body than the good pleasure of God. The world promises passing rewards of little worth, and is served with great eagerness; I promise eternal and rich rewards, yet the hearts of men are indifferent to them. Who is there who serves and obeys Me with as great devotion as he serves the world and its rulers? 'Be ashamed, O Sidon,' cries the sea; and if you ask the reason, hear why.

For a small reward a man will hurry away on a long journey, while for eternal life many will hardly take a single step. Men seek petty gains; they will quarrel shamefully over a single coin; for a mere trifle or vague promise they will toil day and night. Oh, the shame of it! For an imperishable good, for a reward beyond all reckoning, for the highest honour and for glory without end, they are unwilling to endure a little toil. O unwilling and complaining servant, shame on you that worldly men are more ready for damnation than you for salvation; for they are more wholehearted in vanity than you in the Truth. They are often deceived in their hopes, but no one is ever deceived in My promises, and I never send away empty any who trusts in Me. What I promise, I give; what I have said, I will perform, provided you remain faithful in My lord to the end. I am the rewarder of all good men, and the mighty vindicator of all the faithful.

Write My words in your heart, and meditate on them earnestly; they will aid you in temptation. Whatever you do not understand when you read, you shall know in the day of My coming. I visit My chosen in two ways; with trial and with consolation. Day by day, I teach them two lessons, one in which I correct their faults, and the other in which I encourage them to progress in virtue. 'He who hears My words and despises them has One who will judge him on the Last Day.'

A Prayer for the Grace of Devotion

THE DISCIPLE. O Lord my God, You are my all and every good. And what am I, that I should presume to address You? I am the poorest of Your servants and a wretched worm, far more poor and worthless than I can ever realize or express. Yet, Lord, remember that I am nothing: I have nothing, and can do nothing. You alone are good, just and holy; You can do all things, fill all things, bestow all things, leaving only the wicked empty-handed. Remember Your mercies, Lord, and fill my heart with Your grace, since it is Your will that none of Your works should be worthless. How can I endure this life of sorrows, unless You strengthen me with Your mercy and grace? Do not turn Your face from me; do not delay Your coming, nor withdraw Your consolation from me, lest my soul become like a waterless desert. Teach me, O Lord, to do Your will; teach me to live worthily and humbly in Your sight; for You are my Wisdom, who know me truly, and who knew me before the world was made, and before I had my being.

CHAPTER 4
On Truth and Humility

CHRIST. My son, walk before Me in truth, and constantly seek Me in simplicity of heart. He who walks before Me in truth shall be protected against the assaults of evil; truth shall deliver him from his deceivers and from the slanders of the wicked. If truth set you free, you are truly free, and need care nothing for the vain words of men.

THE DISCIPLE. Lord, this is true; let it be as you have said. Let Your truth be my teacher and my guard, and lead me to salvation in the end. Let it free me from every evil affection and lawless love, and I will walk before You in complete freedom of heart.

CHRIST. I will teach you, says the Truth, what is pleasing to Me. Remember your sins with deep sorrow and displeasure, and never think yourself to be anything because of your good deeds. Remember that you are a sinner, entangled and enchained by many passions. Of yourself, you always tend to nothing; you quickly fail, and are overcome; you are soon disturbed and overthrown. You have nothing of which to boast, but many things of which to be ashamed, for you are much weaker than you realize.

Let nothing that you have achieved seem of great importance. Let nothing seem great, precious or admirable to you; nothing worthy of regard, nothing high, praiseworthy or desirable, save that which is everlasting. Let the eternal Truth be your sole and supreme joy, and let your own deep unworthiness always distress you. Nothing should be more feared, condemned, and shunned than your own sins and vices; these should cause you more distress than the loss of everything. Some do not live sincerely in My sight, but, moved by curiosity and conceit, wish to know My secrets and to fathom the high mysteries of God, while neglecting the salvation of their own souls. When I refuse them, such men often fall into great temptations and sins through pride and curiosity.

Stand in awe of God's judgement, and fear the anger of Almighty God. Do not presume to investigate the ways of the Most High, but rather examine yourself, see how greatly you have sinned, and how much good you have left undone. Some carry their devotion only in books, pictures, and other visible signs and representations. Some have Me on their lips, but seldom in their hearts. There are others who are enlightened in mind and pure in affection, who long always for the things of heaven. These listen with reluctance to worldly matters, and grudge even to serve their bodily needs. They fully understand what the Spirit of Truth speaks within them. For He teaches them to despise earthly things and to love heavenly; to forsake this world, and to long for Heaven.

CHAPTER 5
On the Wonderful Effect of Divine Love

THE DISCIPLE. O Heavenly Father, Father of my Lord Jesus Christ, blessed be Your Name for ever, for You have deigned to consider me, the poorest of Your servants. Father of mercies and God of all comfort, I thank You that, unworthy as I am, You sometimes refresh me with Your consolation. Blessing and glory to You, with Your sole-begotten Son and with the Holy Spirit the Comforter, now and through endless ages. You are my glory, and the joy of my heart; for You are my hope, and my refuge in time of trouble.

As yet my love is weak, and my virtue imperfect, and I have great need of Your strength and comfort. Therefore, visit me often, I pray, and instruct me in Your holy laws. Set me free from evil passions, and heal my heart from all disorderly affections; that, healed and cleansed in spirit, I may grow able to love, strong to endure, and steadfast to persevere.

Love is a mighty power, a great and complete good; Love alone lightens every burden, and makes the rough places smooth. It bears every hardship as though it were nothing, and renders all bitterness sweet and acceptable. The love of Jesus is noble, and inspires us to great deeds; it moves us always to desire perfection. Love aspires to high things, and is held back by nothing base. Love longs to be free, a stranger to every worldly desire, lest its inner vision become dimmed, and lest worldly self-interest hinder it or ill-fortune cast it down. Nothing is sweeter than love, nothing stronger, nothing higher, nothing wider, nothing more pleasant, nothing fuller or better in heaven or earth; for love is born of God, and can rest only in God, above all created things.

Love flies, runs, and leaps for joy; it is free and unrestrained. Love gives all for all, resting in One who is highest above all things, from whom every good flows and proceeds. Love does not regard the gifts, but turns to the Giver of all good gifts. Love knows no limits, but ardently transcends all bounds. Love feels no burden, takes no account of toil, attempts things beyond its strength; love sees nothing as impossible, for it feels able to achieve all things. Love therefore does great things; it is strange and effective; while he who lacks love faints and fails.

Love is watchful, and while resting, never sleeps; weary, it is never exhausted; imprisoned, it is never in bonds; alarmed, it is never afraid; like a living flame and a burning torch, it surges upward and surely surmounts every obstacle. Whoever loves God knows well the sound of His voice. A loud cry in the ears of God is that burning love of the soul which exclaims, 'My God and my love, You are all mine, and I am Yours.'

A Prayer

Deepen Your love in me, O Lord, that I may learn in my inmost heart how sweet it is to love, to be dissolved, and to plunge myself into Your love. Let Your love possess and raise me above myself, with a fervour and wonder beyond imagination. Let me sing the song of love. Let me follow You, my Beloved, into the heights. Let my soul spend itself in Your praise, rejoicing for love. Let me love You more than myself, and myself only for Your own sake. Let me love all men who truly love You, as the law of love commands, which shines out from You.

Love is swift, pure, tender, joyful, and pleasant. Love is strong, patient, faithful, prudent, long-suffering, vigorous, and never self-seeking. For when a man is self-seeking he abandons love. Love is watchful, humble, and upright; Love is not fickle and sentimental, nor is it intent on vanities. It is sober, pure, steadfast, quiet, and guarded in all the senses. Love is submissive and obedient to superiors, mean and contemptible in its own sight, devoted and thankful to God, trusting and hoping in Him even when not enjoying His sweetness; for none can live in love without suffering.

Whoever is not prepared to endure everything, and to stand firmly by the will of the Beloved, is not worthy to be called a lover. A lover must willingly accept every hardship and bitterness for the sake of his Beloved, and must never desert Him because of adversity.

CHAPTER 6
On the Proof of a True Lover

CHRIST. My son, you are not yet a brave and wise lover.
THE DISCIPLE. Why, Lord?

CHRIST. Because as soon as you encounter a little trouble, you abandon what you have begun, and eagerly seek for comfort. A brave lover stands firm in temptation, and pays no heed to the crafty arguments of the Devil. He is as true to Me in trouble as in prosperity.

A wise lover values not so much the gift of the lover, as the love of the giver. He esteems the affection above the gift, and values every gift far below the Beloved. A noble lover is not content with a gift, but desires Myself above all gifts. All is not lost, therefore, if sometimes you do not feel that devotion to Me and My Saints that you desire. The good and pleasant affection which you sometimes enjoy is the effect of My grace in you, and is a foretaste of your heavenly home; but do not rely on it too much, for it comes and goes. To fight against evil thoughts as they occur, and to reject with scorn the suggestions of the Devil, is a noteworthy sign of virtue and merit.

Let no strange fancies disturb you, from whatever source they spring. Hold to your purpose bravely, and keep an upright intent towards God. It is no illusion if you are sometimes rapt out of yourself, yet swiftly return to the usual trivial thoughts of men. For these are involuntary rather than deliberate, and as long as they do not please you, can be turned to your gain and not your loss.

You may be sure that the old Enemy is working by every means to frustrate your desire for good, and to entice you away from every spiritual exercise of devotion; from veneration of the Saints, from devout

CITY AND ISLINGTON
SIXTH FORM COLLEGE
283 - 309 GOSWELL ROAD
LONDON

meditation on My Passion, from profitable examination of your sins, from the guard of your heart, and
from the firm resolve to grow in holiness. He suggests
many evil thoughts to discourage you, and to draw
you away from holy reading and prayer. Humble
Confession is hateful to him, and if he could, he would
make you give up Communion. Do not listen to him
or believe him, however often he tries to entrap you.
Charge him with it, when he suggests evil and unholy
things. Say to him, 'Away, unclean spirit! Blush for
shame, wretch! You are foul indeed to speak of these
things! Off with you, most evil of liars! You shall have
no part in me. Jesus will be with me like a mighty
warrior, and you will stand confounded. I would
rather die and suffer any torture than consent to you.
Be silent, and shut your mouth! I will listen to you no
longer, however often you pester me.' 'The Lord is
my light and my salvation: whom shall I fear?' 'Though
a host should encamp against me, my heart shall not
be afraid.' 'The Lord is my helper and redeemer.'

Give battle, like a good soldier, and if through
weakness you sometimes fall, take greater strength
than before and put your trust in My more abundant
grace. Be also on your guard against vain complacency
and conceit, for this leads many into error, and causes
almost incurable blindness of heart. Let the overthrow
of the proud, who presumed in their own strength,
be a warning to you and keep you always humble.

CHAPTER 7
On Concealing Grace under Humility

CHRIST. My son, it is safer and better for you to conceal the grace of devotion; do not boast of it, do not speak much of it, and do not dwell much on it. It is better to think the more humbly of yourself, and to fear that this grace has been granted to one who is unworthy of it. Never depend too much on these feelings, for they may be rapidly changed to the opposite. When you enjoy such grace, consider how sad and needy you are without it. Progress in the spiritual life consists not so much in enjoying the grace of consolation, as in bearing its withdrawal with humility, resignation and patience, neither growing weary in prayer nor neglecting your other acts of devotion. Do willingly, and to the best of your ability and understanding, whatever lies in your power, and do not neglect your spiritual life because of any dryness or anxiety of mind.

There are many who grow impatient or indolent when all does not go according to their wishes. But man's life is not always in his control; it belongs to God alone to give and to comfort when He wills, as much as He wills, and whom He wills, just as He pleases and no more. Some people, lacking discretion, have brought ruin on themselves through the grace of devotion, attempting more than lay in their power, ignoring the measure of their own littleness, and following the promptings of the heart rather than the dictates of reason. And because they presumed to greater things than pleased God, they soon lost His grace. These souls, who aspired to build their nest in Heaven, became needy and wretched outcasts, in order that, through humiliation and poverty, they might learn not to fly with their own wings, but to trust themselves under My wings. For those who are still new and untried in the Way of the Lord can easily be deceived and lost, unless they are guided by wise counsel.

If they follow their own notions rather than trust others of proved experience, their end will be perilous unless they are willing to be drawn away from their own conceit. Those who are wise in their own conceit seldom humbly accept guidance from others. A little knowledge and understanding tempered by humility is better than a great store of learning coupled with vain complacency. It is better to have few talents than many of which you might be conceited. Whoever yields himself to joy, forgetful of his former poverty, is very unwise, for he forgets also that pure reverence for the Lord which fears to lose grace already given. Nor is he wise who, in trouble and adversity, yields to despair, and fails to put his trust in Me.

The man who feels secure in time of peace, will often in time of war be found discouraged and afraid. If you were careful to remain always humble and modest in your own esteem, and to direct and control your mind rightly, you would not fall so readily into danger and disgrace. It is good advice, that when the spirit of devotion is aflame in your heart, you should consider how you will fare when the light leaves you.

When this happens, remember that this light will one day return, which I have now for a while withdrawn as a warning to you and for My glory.

Such a trial is often more profitable than if all went agreeably with you, and in accordance with your wishes. For a man's merit is not to be reckoned by the visions and comforts he may enjoy, nor by his learning in the Scriptures, nor by his being raised to high dignity. Rather is it by his being grounded in humility and filled with divine love; by his pure, constant, and sincere seeking of God's glory; by his low esteem and honest depreciation of himself; and by his preference for humiliation and despite rather than honours at the hands of men.

[. . .]

CHAPTER 9
How God Alone is our True End

CHRIST. My son, I must be your supreme and final End, if you desire true happiness. Fixed on Myself, your affection which too often is wrongly inclined to yourself and creatures, will be cleansed. For whenever you seek yourself, at once you become discouraged and desolate. Therefore, refer all things to Me, for it is I who have given all to you. Consider everything as springing from the supreme Good, since to Myself, as their Source, must all things return.

From Myself, as from a living fountain, both small

and great, rich and poor alike draw the water of life; and they who freely and willingly serve Me, shall receive grace upon grace. But whoever desires to glory in anything outside Me, or to delight in some personal good thing, will not be established in true joy, nor uplifted in heart, but will be hindered and frustrated in countless ways. Therefore, ascribe no good to yourself, nor to any man, but ascribe all to God, without whom man has nothing. I have given all, and it is My will that all return to Me again; I shall require a grateful and exact account.

This, then, is the truth, by which vainglory is put to flight. And if heavenly grace and true charity enter in, there will be no envy or meanness of heart, nor will self-love retain possession. Divine charity overcomes everything, enlarging every power of the soul. If you are truly wise, you will rejoice and hope in Me alone; for none is good but God alone, who is to be praised above all, and to be blessed in all.

CHAPTER 10

On the Joy of God's Service

THE DISCIPLE. Lord, I will speak once more; I cannot remain silent. I will say to my God, my Lord and my King, who dwells on high, 'Oh, how great and manifold are Your joys, kept in secret for those who fear You.' But what are You to those who love You? What to those who serve You with their whole heart? The contemplation of Yourself is the ineffable sweet-

ness that You grant to those who love You. And this
is the supreme manifestation of Your love, that when
I had no being, You created me; when I went astray,
You led me back to Your service, and taught me to
love You.

O Fount of eternal love, what may I say of You?
How can I forget You, who have deigned to remember
me, even after I was corrupted and lost? You have
showed mercy on Your servant beyond all my hope;
You have given grace and friendship beyond all my
deserts. What return can I make to You for this grace?
For it is not granted to all men to forsake everything,
to renounce the world, and to enter the life of religion.
And is it a great thing that I should serve You, whom
all creation is bound to serve? It should not seem
much to me that I should serve you; rather is it great
and wonderful to me that You should see fit to receive
into Your service one so poor and unworthy, and
count him among Your beloved servants.

All that I have is Yours, and myself with it. Yet it is
really You who serve me, rather than I You. Heaven
and earth, which You created for the use of man,
await Your pleasure, and obey Your laws day by day.
And even this is little, for You have appointed the very
Angels to minister to men. But what surpasses all
these, is that You Yourself stoop to serve man, and
have promised him the gift of Yourself.

What return can I make for all these countless
favours? If only I could serve You faithfully all the
days of my life! If only I could render You worthy
service, even for a single day! For You alone are

worthy of all service, honour, and eternal praise. You are truly my God, and I Your poor servant, who am bound to serve with all my powers, nor should I ever weary in Your praise. This is my wish and desire; whatever is lacking in me, I pray You to supply.

It is a great honour and glory to serve you, and to despise all else for Your sake; for great grace will be given to those who have willingly entered Your most holy service. They will discover the sweetest consolations of the Holy Spirit, who for Your love have renounced all the delights of the flesh. They will win true freedom of mind, who for Your Name's sake have entered on the narrow way, and set aside all worldly interests.

O gracious and joyful service of God, in which man is made truly free and holy! O sacred state of religious service, which makes man the equal of Angels, pleasing to God, terrible to devils, and an example to all the faithful! O most lovely and desirable service, in which we receive the reward of the supreme Good, and obtain the joy that abides for ever!

CHAPTER II
On Control of the Heart

CHRIST. My son, you have still many things to learn.
THE DISCIPLE. What are these, Lord?
CHRIST. How you must frame your desires in accordance with My good pleasure, and be not a lover of self, but an earnest follower of My will. Desires often

inflame you and drive you violently onwards; but consider whether it be My honour or self-interest that moves you most. If I Myself be the cause, you will be content with whatever I shall determine; but if self-interest is your hidden motive, this will be a hindrance and burden to you.

Take care, therefore, not to rely overmuch on any preconceived desire without asking My counsel, lest you regret or become displeased at what first pleased you, and for which you were eager. For not every feeling that seems good is at once to be acted upon, nor is every feeling that runs contrary to your inclinations to be immediately rejected. It is sometimes necessary to restrain even your good intentions and endeavours, lest by over-eagerness your mind becomes distracted; lest by lack of discipline you cause offence to others; or lest you suddenly become confused and upset by the opposition of others.

You must bravely and forcibly resist your sensual appetite, taking no account of what the body likes or dislikes, and struggle to subdue the unwilling flesh to the spirit. For it must be corrected and brought under control, until it is obedient in everything. It must learn to be content with little, to take pleasure in simple things, and not to complain at any hardship.

CHAPTER 12
On Learning Patience

THE DISCIPLE. O Lord God, I know that I need patience above all else, for in this life there are many trials. For however earnestly I seek peace, I cannot escape struggle and sorrow.

CHRIST. This is true, My son. But My will is that you do not try to find a place free from temptations and troubles. Rather, seek a peace that endures even when you are beset by various temptations and tried by much adversity. If you say that you cannot endure much, how will you endure the fires of Purgatory? Of two evils, always choose the lesser. Endeavour patiently to endure for God's sake all the ills of this life, that you may escape eternal punishment. Do you imagine that worldly men suffer little or nothing? Ask the most wealthy, and you will not find it so.

But, you may say, they enjoy many pleasures, and follow their own desires; in this way they make light of any troubles. Yet, even if they enjoy whatever they desire, how long will this last? The rich of this world will vanish like smoke, and no memory of their past pleasures will remain. But even in their lifetime they do not enjoy them without bitterness, weariness and fear, for the very things whence they derive their pleasures often carry with them the seeds of sorrow. And this is but just; for having sought and followed pleasures to excess, they may not enjoy them without shame and bitterness. Ah, how short-lived and false, how disorderly and base are all these pleasures! Yet so besotted and blind are such persons that, like dumb beasts, they bring death to their souls for the trivial enjoyments of this corruptible life! My son, do not follow your lusts, and do not be self-willed. Delight in the Lord, and he will grant your heart's desire.

If you would taste true pleasure and receive the fullness of My consolation, know this: that in the despising of worldly things and in the shunning of base delights shall be your blessing, and you shall win abundant consolation. The more you withdraw yourself from the comfort of creatures, the sweeter and more potent will be the consolations that you will find in Me. But you will not find these at once, or without sorrow, toil and effort. Old habits will stand in your way, but by better they will be overcome. The body will complain, but by fervour of the spirit it can be disciplined. The Old Serpent will goad and disturb you, but by prayer he will be put to flight; and by profitable labour you will bar the wide path by which he comes to attack you.

CHAPTER 13
On Obedience, after the Example of Christ

CHRIST. My son, whoever strives to withdraw from obedience, withdraws from grace. And he who seeks personal privileges, loses those that are common to all. When a man is unwilling to submit freely and willingly to his superior, it is a sign that his lower nature is not yet under his control, but frequently rebels and complains. Therefore learn to obey your superior promptly if you wish to subdue your lower nature, for the Enemy without is sooner overcome if our inner fortress remains intact. There is no enemy more wicked or troublesome to the soul than yourself, when you are not in harmony with the Spirit, and you must have a very real scorn for self, if you are to prevail against flesh and Blood. It is because you are unwilling to yield your will to that of others, that you are still full of self-love.

Is it so hard for you, who are dust and nothingness, to subject yourself to man for God's sake, when I, the Almighty and most high, who created all things from nothing, humbly subjected Myself to man for your sake? I became the humblest and least of all men, that you might overcome your pride through My humility. Learn to obey, you who are but dust; learn to humble yourself, earth and clay, and to bow yourself beneath the feet of all. Learn to curb your desires, and yield yourself to complete obedience.

Direct your anger against yourself, and let no swelling pride remain in you. Show yourself so submissive and so humble that all men may trample over you and tread on you like the mud of the streets. Vain man, what right have you to complain? What can you, an unclean sinner, answer to any who reproach you, when you have so often offended God, and so many times deserved Hell? But I have spared you, for your soul was precious to Me, that you might know My love, and be ever grateful for My favour: also, that you might give yourself constantly to true obedience and humility, enduring patiently any contempt laid on you.

[. . .]

CHAPTER 17

How we must put our Whole Trust in God

CHRIST. My son, let My will be your guide. I know what is best for you. Your mind is but human, and your judgement often influenced by personal considerations.

THE DISCIPLE. Lord, this is true, and Your providence will order my life better than I can myself: most insecure is the man who does not put all his trust in You. Lord, keep my will steadfast and true to You, and do with me whatever is Your pleasure; for all is good that comes to me by Your will. If You will that darkness be my lot, blessed be Your Name; if it be light, again blessed be Your Name. If You stoop to comfort me, blessed be Your Name; and if You wish to try me, ever blessed be Your Name.

CHRIST. My son, let this be your disposition if you wish to walk with Me. Be as ready to suffer as to be glad; be as willing to be needy and poor as to enjoy wealth and plenty.

THE DISCIPLE. Lord, for Your sake I will gladly bear whatever You shall send to me. From Your hand I will accept gladly both good and ill, sweet and bitter, joy and sorrow; and for all that may befall me, I will thank You. Only keep me, O Lord, from all sin, and I shall fear neither Death nor Hell. Do not, I pray, reject me for ever, nor blot out my name from the book of life; then, whatever trials beset me can do me no harm.

CHAPTER 18
How Sorrows are to be Borne Patiently

CHRIST. My son, I came down from Heaven for your salvation. I took upon Myself your sorrows, not because I must, but out of pure love, that you might learn patience, and bear without complaint all the troubles of this world. From the hour of My Birth until My Death on the Cross, I had always to endure sorrow. I suffered great lack of worldly goods; many accusations were levelled against Me. I bore all disgrace and insults with meekness. In return for blessings I received ingratitude; for miracles, blasphemies; for My teaching, reproofs.

THE DISCIPLE. Lord, because You were patient in Your life, in this respect especially fulfilling the command of Your Father, it is fitting that I, a wretched sinner, should bear myself patiently in accordance with Your will, and that, for the salvation of my soul, I should bear the burden of this corruptible life so long as You shall will. For though this present life is hard, yet by Your grace it is made full of merit; and by Your example and the lives of Your Saints it is rendered easier and happier for the weak. Its consolations are richer than under the old Law, when the gates of Heaven were shut, and the way thither dark, so that few cared to enter the Kingdom of Heaven. And even those who in former days were righteous and to be saved could not enter the Kingdom of Heaven until Your Passion and the Atonement of Your sacred Death.

What boundless gratitude is Your due, for revealing to me and to all faithful people the true and holy way to Your eternal Kingdom! Your life is Our Way, and by holy patience we will journey onwards to You, who are our crown and consummation. If You, Lord, had not gone before us and showed the way, who could follow? How many would have stayed behind and far distant had they not Your glorious example for their guide? Even now we are cold and careless, although we have heard Your teaching and mighty acts; what would happen to us had we not Your light as our guide?

CHAPTER 19
On Enduring Injuries, and the Proof of Patience

CHRIST. My son, what are you saying? Consider My sufferings and those of My Saints, and cease to complain. You have not yet shed your blood in resistance; your troubles are but small in comparison with those who have suffered so much, whose temptations were so strong, whose trials so severe, and who were proved and tested in so many ways. Remember the heavier sufferings of others, that you may more easily bear your own small troubles. If they do not seem small to you, beware lest your impatience be the cause; and whether they be small or great, try to bear them all patiently.

The better you prepare yourself to meet suffering, the more wisely will you act, and the greater will be your merit. You will bear all more easily if your heart and mind is diligently prepared. Do not say, 'I cannot endure such things from this person,' or, 'I will not tolerate these things: he has done me great injury, and accused me of things I never considered; from another person I might bear it, and regard it as something that must be endured.' Such thoughts are foolish, for you ignore the merit of patience and Him who rewards it, and think only of the person who has injured you and the wrong you endure.

You are not truly patient if you will only endure what you think fit, and only from those whom you like. A truly patient man does not consider by whom he is tried, whether by his superior, his equal, or his inferior; whether by a good and holy man, or by a perverse and wicked person. But however great or frequent the trial that besets him, and by whatever agency it comes, he accepts it gladly as from the hand of God, and counts it all gain.

Always be ready for battle if you wish for victory; you cannot win the crown of patience without a struggle; if you refuse to suffer, you refuse the crown. Therefore, if you desire the crown, fight manfully and endure patiently. Without labour, no rest is won; without battle, there can be no victory.

THE DISCIPLE. Lord, make possible for me by grace what is impossible to me by nature. You know how little I can bear, and how quickly I become discouraged by a little adversity. I pray You, make every trial lovely and desirable to me for Your Name's sake, since suffering and affliction for Your sake is so profitable to the health of my soul.

CHAPTER 20
On our own Weakness, and the Trials of This Life

THE DISCIPLE. Lord, I confess my sinfulness, and acknowledge my weakness. Often it is but a small matter that defeats and troubles me. I resolve to act boldly, but when I am assailed even by a small temptation, I am in sore straits. From a trifling thing sometimes arises a strong temptation; and when I think I am secure, I am almost overwhelmed by a mere breath.

Consider my lowness and weakness, O Lord, for You know all things. Have mercy on me, and raise me from the mire, that I may not stick fast in it, nor remain prostrate. It is this that often defeats and confounds me in Your eyes – that I am so prone to fall and so weak in resisting my passions. And although I do not yield to them entirely, yet their assaults trouble and distress me, so that I am weary of living constantly at conflict. My weakness is apparent to me, for evil fancies rush in on me more readily than they depart.

Most mighty God of Israel, zealous lover of souls, I pray You remember the toil and grief of Your servant, and support him in all his undertakings. Strengthen me with heavenly courage, lest my old and wicked enemy the flesh, not yet wholly subject to the spirit, prevail and gain the upper hand. For against this I must fight while breath remains in this troublous life. Alas, what a life is this, where trials and sorrows never cease, and where all things are full of snares and foes! For when one trial or temptation departs, another takes its place; and even while the conflict rages, other troubles arise, innumerable and unexpected.

How can we love life, when it holds so much bitterness, and is subject to so many sorrows and calamities? How, indeed, can that be called life, which breeds death and pain in such full measure? Yet it is loved, and many find great delight in it. The world is often blamed for its falseness and vanity, but it is not readily abandoned: the desires of the body exercise too strong a hold. Some things cause us to love the world, others to hate it. The desires of the body, the desires of the eyes, and the pride of life all draw us to love the world; but the pains and sorrows that justly ensue cause us to hate and weary of it.

Alas, a perverted pleasure overcomes the mind that surrenders to the world, and counts it a delight to lie among the brambles, for it has neither seen nor tasted the sweetness of God and the inner joy of holiness. But they who perfectly despise the world and study to live under God's holy rule know something of that heavenly sweetness promised to all who sincerely forsake the world. They see most clearly how sadly the world goes astray, and how grievously it is deceived.

CHAPTER 21
How we must Rest in God Alone above all Things

THE DISCIPLE. Above all things and in all things rest always in the Lord, O my soul, for He is the everlasting rest of the Saints.

A Prayer

Grant me, most dear and loving Jesus, to rest in You above created things; above health and beauty, above all glory and honour; above all power and dignity, above all knowledge and skill; above all fame and praise, above all sweetness and consolation; above all hope and promise, above all merit and desire; above all gifts and favours that You can bestow and shower upon us; above all joy and jubilation that the mind can conceive and know; above Angels and Archangels and all the hosts of Heaven; above all things visible and invisible; and above everything that is not Yourself, O my God.

O Lord my God, You transcend all things; You alone are most high, most mighty, most sufficient and complete, most sweet and comforting. You alone are most full of beauty and glory, in Whom all good things in their perfection exist, both now and ever have been, and ever will be. All, therefore, is too small and unsatisfying that You can give me beside Yourself, or that You can reveal and promise me of Yourself unless I can see and fully possess You. For my heart cannot rest nor be wholly content until it rests in You, rising above all Your gifts and creatures.

O Lord Jesus Christ, spouse of the soul, lover of purity, and Lord of creation, who will give me wings of perfect liberty, that I may fly to You, and be at rest? When shall I be set free, and taste Your sweetness, O Lord my God? When shall I become recollected in You, that for love of You I may no longer be conscious of myself, but of You alone in a manner not known to all men, and above all perception and measure? But now I mourn and bear my unhappy lot with grief, for many evils happen in this vale of sorrows, which often disturb, sadden and darken my path. They often hinder and distract, entice, and entangle me, so that I cannot approach You freely, nor yet enjoy the sweet embrace which You prepare for the souls of the blessed.

O Jesus, Brightness of eternal glory and comfort of the pilgrim soul, hear my cry, and regard my utter desolation. Words fail me in Your presence; let my silence speak for me. How long will my Lord delay His coming? Come to me, Lord, poor and little as I am, and bring me joy. Stretch out Your hand, and deliver me from all my misery and pain. Come, Lord, come, for without You no day or hour is happy; without You my table is without its guest, for You alone are my joy. Sadness is my lot, and I am like a man imprisoned and loaded with chains, until You refresh me with the light of Your presence, and show me Your face as my friend. Let others seek whom they will besides You, but nothing ever can or will give me joy but Yourself alone, my God, my Hope, and my eternal Salvation. I will not keep silent, nor cease from urgent prayer till Your grace returns and my heart leaps at the sound of Your voice.

CHRIST. See, I am here. I have come at your cry. Your tears and your soul's longing, your humiliation and contrition of heart have moved Me to come to you.

THE DISCIPLE. Lord, I have called You and longed for You. I am ready to renounce everything for Your sake, who first moved me to seek You. Blessed be Your Name, O Lord, for Your goodness to Your servant, according to the richness of Your mercies. What more can Your servant say, Lord? He can only humble himself entirely in Your presence, ever mindful of his own wickedness and unworthiness. For none can compare with You, among all the wonders of heaven and earth. All Your works are good, Your judgements are true, and by Your providence are all things ruled. Praise and glory to You, O Wisdom of the Father! Let my soul, my lips, and all creation join in Your blessing and Your praise!

[. . .]

CHAPTER 23
On Four Things that Bring Peace

CHRIST. My son, I will now teach you the way of peace and true freedom.

THE DISCIPLE. Lord, instruct me, I pray. I am eager to learn.

CHRIST. My son, resolve to do the will of others rather than your own.

Always choose to possess less rather than more.

Always take the lowest place, and regard yourself as less than others.

Desire and pray always that God's will may be perfectly fulfilled in you.

A man who observes these rules shall come to enjoy peace and tranquillity of soul.

THE DISCIPLE. Lord, in these few words of Yours lie the whole secret of perfection. If I could only faithfully observe them, no trouble could distress me. For whenever I am anxious and weary, I find that it is because I have strayed from Your teaching. All things are in Your power, and You always long to bring souls to perfection. Give me Your grace ever more richly; help me to keep Your word and advance my salvation.

A Prayer against Evil Thoughts

My Lord and God, do not abandon me; remember my need, for many evil thoughts and horrid fears trouble my mind and terrify my soul. How shall I pass through them unhurt? How shall I break their power over me? You have said, 'I will go before you, and will humble the proud upon earth. I will open the gates of the prison, and reveal to you the hidden treasures and secrets of the ages.' Do, O Lord, as You have said, and let Your coming put to flight all wicked thoughts. It is my hope and comfort that I can turn to You in all my troubles, put my trust in You, call upon You in my heart, and wait Your comfort in patience.

A Prayer for Mental Light

O merciful Jesus, send the brightness of Your light into my mind, and banish all darkness from the sanctuary of my heart. Restrain my many wayward thoughts, and destroy the temptations that beset me with such violence. Let Your great strength be with me in the fight, and overcome the seducing desires of the flesh, that rage in me like evil beasts. By Your power establish peace, and let Your praises be sung in the temple of a pure heart. Command the winds and storm; subdue the fury of the seas and the blast of the north wind, and there shall be a great calm. Send out Your light and Your truth to shine over the world; for until Your light illuminates my soul, I am dull earth, formless and empty. Pour forth Your grace from above, and bathe my heart in the dew of Heaven. Supply fresh streams of devotion to water the face of the earth, and produce good and perfect fruit. Inspire my mind, now burdened by my sins, and fix my whole desire on heavenly things, so that, having once tasted the sweetness of eternal joys, I may turn with distaste from all the passing pleasures of this world. Release me, and free my heart from all dependence on the passing consolation of wicked things, since none of these things can yield true satisfaction or appease my longings. Unite me to Yourself by the unbreakable bonds of love. You alone can satisfy the soul that loves You, and without You the world is worthless.

CHAPTER 24
On the Evils of Curiosity

CHRIST. Beware of vain curiosity, My son, and do not busy yourself in profitless matters; what are they to you? Follow Me. What concern is it of yours whether a man is good or evil, or what he says and does? You will not be called on to answer for others, but you will certainly have to give a full account of your own life. Why, then, must you meddle where you have no need? I know the hearts of all men, and nothing under the sun is hid from My knowledge. I know the life of every man – his thoughts, his desires and his intentions. Therefore trust yourself entirely to My care, and let your heart be at peace. Let the meddlesome man trouble himself as he will; his words and deeds will recoil on his own head, for he cannot deceive Me.

Do not court the favour of powerful patrons, nor popular favour, not even the particular affection of friends. All these things are distractions, and fill the heart with uncertainty. If you will but await My coming, and throw open the door of your heart, I Myself will speak to you, and reveal to you My secrets. Be ready; watch and pray. Above all, be humble.

CHAPTER 25
On Lasting Peace and True Progress

CHRIST. I have said, 'Peace I leave with you; My own peace I give you. Not as the world gives do I give you.' All men want peace, but all do not seek those things that bring true peace. My peace is with the humble and gentle of heart, and depends on great patience. If you listen to Me, and follow My words, you shall find true peace.

THE DISCIPLE. What must I do, Lord?

CHRIST. Keep guard over your whole life, your actions and words. Direct all your efforts to the single purpose of pleasing Me: seek and desire Myself alone. Never make rash judgements on the behaviour of others, and do not interfere when your opinion is not sought. If you do as I say, you will seldom be troubled in mind. But do not imagine that you can avoid anxiety in this life, or that you may never experience sorrow of heart or pain of body, for true peace is only to be found in the state of eternal rest. So do not think that you have found true peace when you happen to experience no trouble, and do not think that all is well when no one opposes you. Nor should you imagine that everything is perfect when everything happens in accordance with your wishes. Do not hold an exaggerated opinion of yourself, or believe that you are a favourite of God when you enjoy the grace of great devotion and sweetness; for it is not by these things that the true lover of holiness is known, or is a man's spiritual progress dependent on such things.

THE DISCIPLE. Lord, on what then does it depend?

CHRIST. On complete surrender of your heart to the will of God, not seeking to have your own way either in great matters or small, in time or in eternity. If you will make this surrender, you will thank God with equal gladness both in good times and in bad, and will accept everything, as from His hand, with an untroubled mind. Be courageous and of such unshakeable faith that, when spiritual comfort is withdrawn, you may prepare your heart for even greater trials. Do not think it unjust that you should suffer so much, but confess that I am just in all My dealings, and praise My holy Name. In so doing, you will walk in the true and noble way of peace, and I will surely come to you again and give you great joy. Only think humbly of yourself, and I promise you as great peace as man may enjoy in this life.

CHAPTER 26
On the Excellence of a Free Mind

THE DISCIPLE. Lord, one who desires perfection must make it his first task to keep his mind at all times set on heavenly things. By so doing, he can pass carefree through many troubles, not as one who has not the wit to realize the dangers that beset him, but in the strength of a free mind, unfettered by undue attachment to worldly things.

Most loving God, I beg You so to preserve me that I am not overborne by the cares of this life. Keep me, also, from becoming the servant of my body's many needs, that I may not become absorbed in its pleasures. Save me from all the pitfalls that beset my soul, that they may not overwhelm and crush me. I do not ask to be preserved from those things that vain and worldly men pursue with such ardour, but rather from those miseries that so heavily burden and impede the soul of Your servant, who lies under the curse common to all mortal men. It is these miseries that prevent my soul from entering into the true liberty of the spirit whenever I would. My Lord God, my Delight above all delights, make bitter to me all worldly pleasure that draws me away from the love of eternal joys, and wickedly seduces me by promising me all the joys of the present. Let me not be overcome by flesh and blood, I entreat You. Let not the world and its brief glory deceive me, nor the Devil and his cunning overthrow me. Give me strength to resist, patience to endure, and constancy to persevere. Give me the rich graces of Your spirit rather than all the pleasures of the world and supplant all worldly love by the love of Your Name. A man of fervent spirit grudges much attention to food, drink, clothing and other bodily needs. Grant me to use these things with moderation, and not to be over-concerned about them. It is not right to ignore them, for nature bids us supply their needs; but the law of holiness forbids us to crave for needless luxuries, since the body then revolts against the spirit. In all things, I pray You, let Your hand guide and govern me, that moderation may be my rule at all times.

[. . .]

CHAPTER 28
Against Slander

CHRIST. My son, do not take it to heart if others think ill of you, and say unpleasant things about you. Consider yourself to be even worse than they imagine, and regard yourself as the weakest of men. If your inner life is strong, you will not pay much heed to passing words. A wise man remains silent when beset by evil; he turns to Me in his heart, and is untroubled by man's judgements.

Do not let your peace depend on what people say of you, for whether they speak good or ill of you makes no difference to what you are. True peace and joy is to be found in Me alone. He who is neither anxious to please nor afraid to displease men enjoys true peace. All unrest of heart and distraction of mind spring from disorderly affections and groundless fears.

CHAPTER 29
How we should Bless God in all Trouble

THE DISCIPLE. Blessed be Your holy Name for ever, O
Lord. I know that it is by Your will that temptation
and trouble come upon me. I cannot escape it, but
must needs come to You for help, that it may be
turned to my good. Lord, I am tormented and uneasy
in mind, and my present troubles weigh heavy on me.
Most loving Father, what may I say? I am in dire
straits. Save me from this hour. Yet it is for Your glory
that I have been brought to this hour, and that I may
learn that You alone can deliver me from the depths
of my humiliation. Of Your goodness, deliver me, O
Lord. For what can I do, helpless as I am; and where
can I go without Your aid? Give me patience, Lord,
even in this trial. Grant me help, and I shall fear
nothing, however hard pressed I may be.

And now, in this trouble, this shall be my prayer,
'Your will be done.' I have fully deserved this trouble,
and must bear it. Let me bear it patiently, until the
storm is past and better days return. I know that Your
almighty power can remove even this trial from me
and lessen its violence, so that I am not completely
crushed by it. Often in times past, my God and my
Mercy, You have done this for me. And the harder it
is for me, the easier it is for You to change my way,
O God most high.

CHAPTER 30
On Asking God's Help, and the Certainty of His Grace

CHRIST. My son, I am the Lord, who gives strength in time of trouble. Come to Me when the struggle goes hard with you. Your slowness in turning to prayer is the greatest obstacle to receiving My heavenly comfort. For, when you should earnestly seek Me, you first turn to many other comforts, and hope to restore yourself by worldly means. It is only when all these things have failed that you remember that I am the Saviour of all who put their trust in Me; and that, apart from Me, there can be no effective help, no sound counsel, and no lasting remedy. But now, with spirit renewed after the tempest, gather fresh strength and light in My mercies. For I am near, and will restore all things, not only completely, but generously and in full measure.

Is anything too hard for Me? Shall I be like one who does not fulfil his promise? Where is your faith? Stand firm, and persevere. Be courageous and patient, and help will come to you in due time. Wait patiently for Me, and I Myself will come and heal you. Temptation is your testing – there is no cause for alarm or fear. Sorrow upon sorrow can be the only result if you worry about the future. Sufficient to the day is the evil in it. It is quite vain and useless to be either anxious or pleased about the future, for what you anticipate may never happen.

The mind of man is prone to delusions, but to be deceived by the suggestions of the Devil is a sign of spiritual weakness. Satan does not care whether it be by truth or falsehood that he mocks and deceives you; or whether he obtains your downfall through love of the present or fear of the future. Therefore, let not your heart be troubled, neither let it be afraid. Trust in Me, and put your whole confidence in My mercy. When you think I am far away, then often I am nearest to you. And when you think the battle almost lost, then the reward of all your toil is often near. All is not lost when anything turns out contrary to your plans. Therefore do not allow your feelings of the moment to obscure your judgement, nor yield to depression as though all hope of recovery were lost.

Do not imagine yourself utterly forsaken if for a while I have allowed some trial to harass you, or withdrawn the comfort that you desire; for this is the way to the Kingdom of Heaven. Be assured that it is better for you, and for all My servants, to struggle against difficulties than to have everything as you wish. I know your secret thoughts, and it is necessary for your salvation that you should sometimes be deprived of spiritual joys, lest you become conceited in your happy state, and complacently imagine yourself better than you are. What I have granted, I can take away, and restore it when I choose.

When I grant comfort, it remains Mine; and when I withdraw it, I am not taking anything that is yours, for every good gift and every perfect gift is Mine alone. If I send you trouble and affliction, do not be indignant or downhearted; for I can swiftly help you, and turn all your sorrow into joy. Notwithstanding, I keep My own counsel, and in all My dealings with you, give Me due praise.

If you are wise and have right judgement, you will never despair or be discouraged. On the contrary, if I scourge you with trouble and do not spare you, be glad and grateful, and regard it as cause for joy. For, 'as My Father has loved Me, so do I love you,' were My words to my well loved disciples, whom I did not send out to enjoy the pleasures of the world, but to fight hard battles; not to win honours, but contempt; not to be idle, but industrious; not to rest, but to bring forth much fruit with patience.

CHAPTER 31
On Forsaking Creatures to Find the Creator

THE DISCIPLE. Lord, I am greatly in need of yet more abundant grace if I am to reach that state where no creature can impede my progress. For as long as anything holds me back, I cannot come freely to You. One who desired to fly freely to You said, 'Who will give me wings like a dove? I will fly, and be at rest.' And who is more perfectly at rest than the man of single purpose? Who more free than he who desires nothing upon earth? Rapt in spirit, a man must rise above all created things, and perfectly forsaking himself, see clearly that nothing in creation can compare with the Creator. But unless a man is freed from dependence on creatures, he cannot turn freely to the things of God. This is the reason why there are so few contemplatives, for there are few who can free themselves entirely from transitory things.

A soul needs much grace to be raised up and carried beyond itself. Yet, unless a man's soul is raised, set free from all attachment to earthly things, and wholly united to God, neither his knowledge nor his possessions are of any value. So long as he esteems as precious anything outside the One, Infinite, and Eternal Good, he will remain mean and earthbound in spirit. For whatever is not God is nothing, and is to be accounted nothing. There is a great difference between the wisdom of a devout man enlightened by God, and the knowledge of a learned and studious scholar. More noble by far is the learning infused from above by divine grace, than that painfully acquired by the industry of man.

Many desire the grace of contemplation, but few take the trouble to practise what is essential to it. It is a great obstacle if we rely on external signs and the experience of the senses, and pay small regard to the perfecting of self-discipline. I hardly know what motives can inspire us, or what our purpose may be, when we who wish to be considered spiritual take so much trouble and are so concerned with trivial, daily affairs, and so seldom give our full and earnest attention to our interior life.

Alas, after a short meditation we break off, and do not make a strict examination of our lives. We do not consider where our affections really lie, nor are we grieved at the sinfulness of our whole life. Yet it was because of the wickedness of men that the Flood came upon the earth. When our inner inclinations are corrupted, the actions that spring from them are also corrupted. And this is a sign of our lack of inner strength; for from a pure heart alone springs the fruit of a holy life.

A man's achievements are often discussed, but seldom the principles by which he lives. We inquire whether he is brave, handsome, rich, clever, a good writer, a fine singer, or a hard worker: but whether he is humble-minded, patient and gentle, devout and spiritual is seldom mentioned. Nature regards the outward characteristics of a man: Grace considers his inner disposition. And while Nature is often misled, Grace trusts in God and cannot be deceived.

CHAPTER 32
On Self-Denial, and Renunciation of our Desires

CHRIST. My son, complete self-denial is the only road to perfect liberty. Those who are obsessed by self-interest and self-love are slaves of their own desires; they are greedy, inquisitive, and discontented. They spend themselves in pleasures, but never in the service of Jesus Christ, their whole interest being in passing affairs. But all that is not of God shall perish utterly. Observe this simple counsel of perfection: Forsake all, and you shall find all. Renounce desire, and you shall find peace. Give this due thought, and when you have put it into practice, you will understand all things.

THE DISCIPLE. Lord, this is not the work of a single day, and no easy matter. These few words contain the whole way of spiritual perfection.

CHRIST. My son, do not be discouraged or diverted from your purpose at hearing of this way of perfection. Rather let it spur you to higher things, and, at least, to set your heart on them. If only you would do this, and attain that state where you cease to be a lover of self, and stand ready to do My will and His whom I have appointed as your Father, you would greatly please Me, and your whole life would be filled with joy and peace. You have still many things to renounce, and unless you surrender them to Me without reserve, you cannot obtain what you ask of Me. I counsel you to buy from Me gold, refined in the fire, that you may be rich in that heavenly wisdom that rejects all worthless things. Despise the wisdom of the world, and every temptation to please others or yourself.

I have said, exchange what men consider desirable and honourable for that which they hold in low esteem. For true heavenly wisdom, having no exalted opinion of itself, seeks no recognition from the world, is almost disregarded by men, and seems to them useless and of no importance. Many pay it lip-service, but it plays no part in their lives. Yet this is the precious pearl, that remains hidden from many.

CHAPTER 33
On Inconstancy of Heart

CHRIST. My son, do not trust your affections, for they are changeable and inconstant. All your life you are subject to change, even against your inclination. At one time you are cheerful, at another sad; now peaceful, now troubled; now full of devotion, now wholly lacking it; now zealous, now slothful; now grave, now gay. But the wise man, who is well versed in spiritual matters, stands above these changing emotions. He pays small regard to his momentary feelings and whims, but directs all the powers of his mind towards the right and true end. Thus, having fixed his gaze and kept his intention constantly on Me, he can remain single in purpose, and unshaken under all circumstances.

The more single his purpose, the more steadily will a man pass through all the storms of life. But in many, this single purpose becomes obscured; for men pay ready attention to any pleasant thing that comes their way, and it is a rare thing to find anyone wholly free from the sin of self-interest. Thus the Jews once came out to Bethany to Martha and Mary, not for Jesus' sake only, but to see Lazarus. Therefore make your intention pure, single, and upright, that it may be directed to Me alone without hindrance.

[. . .]

CHAPTER 36
Against the Vain Judgements of Men

CHRIST. My son, trust in God with all your heart. If your conscience bears witness to your devotion and innocence, you need not fear the judgements of men. It is a good and holy thing to suffer in this way, and it will not be a burden to the humble heart that trusts in God rather than itself. Many people talk too much, and little attention should be paid them. Moreover, it is quite impossible to please everyone. Although Saint Paul endeavoured to be pleasing to all men in the Lord, and became all things to all men, yet he cared very little what they thought of himself. He did whatever lay in his power to bring instruction and salvation to others, but even he could not escape being misjudged and despised by others. Accordingly he trusted himself wholly to God, who knows all things, and opposed the shield of patience and humility to the unjust accusations, empty lies and vain boasts of his detractors. Notwithstanding, sometimes he replied to them, lest his silence should give scandal to the weak.

Why should you fear mortal man? Today he is here; tomorrow he is gone for ever. Fear God, and you need never fear man. What real harm can the words or actions of any man do you? He injures himself rather than you, and he cannot escape the judgement of God, whoever he be. Keep God always before you, and do not engage in bitter controversies. Even if for the present you seem to suffer defeat and undeserved disgrace, do not complain nor lessen your due reward through impatience. Instead, raise your eyes to Me in Heaven, for I have power to deliver you from all shame and wrong, and to reward every man according to his merits.

CHAPTER 37

How Surrender of Self Brings Freedom of Heart

CHRIST. My son, renounce self, and you shall find Me. Retain no private choice or personal interest, and you will always be the gainer. As soon as you yield yourself unreservedly into My hands, I will grant you even richer graces.

THE DISCIPLE. How often shall I yield myself, and in what way forsake myself, Lord?

CHRIST. Always, and at all times, in small things as well as in great. I make no exceptions, for I desire to have you wholly divested of self: otherwise, unless you are wholly stripped of self-will, how can you be Mine, or I yours? The sooner you do this, the better it will be with you, and the more completely and sincerely you do it, the better you will please Me, and the greater will be your gain.

Some resign themselves, but with some reservation; these do not put their whole trust in God, and are therefore concerned to provide for themselves. Others at first offer everything, but later are overcome by temptation, and return to their former state. These make very little progress in virtue, and will never

obtain the true freedom of heart, nor enjoy the favour
of My friendship, unless they first make a complete
surrender and daily offering of themselves to Me.
Without this, no fruitful union with Me can exist or
endure.

I have often said to you, and I now say once more:
Renounce yourself, surrender yourself, and you shall
enjoy great inner peace. Give all for all, look for
nothing, ask nothing in return: rest purely and trust-
ingly in Me, and you shall possess Me. Then you will
be free in heart, and no darkness will oppress your
soul. Strive for this, pray for this, desire this one thing
– that you may be stripped clean of all selfishness, and
follow Jesus in complete self-abandonment, dying to
self that you may live to Me for ever. Then will all
vain fantasies be put to flight, and all evil disorders
and groundless fears vanish. Then will all fear and
dread depart, and all disordered love die in you.

CHAPTER 38
On the Right Ordering of our Affairs

CHRIST. My son, take great care to ensure that in every
place, action, and outward occupation you remain
inwardly free and your own master. Control circumstances, and do not allow them to control you. Only
so can you be master and ruler of your actions, not
their servant or slave; a free man and a true Christian,
enjoying the freedom and high destiny of the children
of God. These stand above the things of time, and

view those of eternity, seeing in their true light both earthly and heavenly things. The things of this world have no hold over the children of God; on the contrary, they draw them into their service, and employ them in the ways ordained by God and established by the Heavenly Architect, who has left nothing in His creation without its due place.

Stand firm in all circumstances. Do not judge by outward appearances or reports as men do, but in each instance enter like Moses into the Tabernacle, to ask guidance of the Lord. Sometimes you will receive God's answer, and return instructed on many matters, both present and future. For Moses always had recourse to the Tabernacle to obtain an answer to his doubts and questions, and he took refuge in prayer to support him amidst the dangers and wickednesses of men. Similarly must you take refuge in the depths of your heart, and pray most earnestly for God's help. We read that Joshua and the children of Israel were deceived by the men of Gibeon because they had not first asked counsel of God. Therefore, in giving credit to their statements, they were misled by their pretended piety.

CHAPTER 39
How we should not be Over Anxious

CHRIST. My son, always commit your cause to Me, and I will bring it to a good issue in due time. Wait until I order it, and you will find it to your advantage.

THE DISCIPLE. Lord, I readily commit everything into your hands, for my own judgement is of small value. I wish I were less concerned about the future, and could unreservedly submit myself to Your good pleasure.

CHRIST. My son, a man often labours incessantly to obtain his desire; but when he has obtained it, he begins to change his mind. For man's affections do not remain constant, but tend to move from one object to another. It is therefore no small advantage, if a man can renounce self even in small things. Man's true spiritual progress depends on the denial of self, and he who renounces self is completely free and secure. But the Old Enemy, the Adversary of all good, never ceases to tempt man. Day and night he lies in ambush, hoping to trap the unwary into the snares of his deceit. 'Watch and pray lest you enter into temptation.'

CHAPTER 40

How Man has no Personal Goodness of which to Boast

THE DISCIPLE. 'Lord, what is man that You are mindful of him, or the son of man, that You visit him?' What has man done to deserve Your grace? Lord, I have no cause to complain if You abandon me; and if Your Will is contrary to my desires, I have no right to plead against it. But this I may rightly think and say, 'Lord, I am nothing and I can do nothing. I have no good of

Myself, but am imperfect in every respect, and always tend to nothing. Unless You guide my soul and grant me strength, I become weak and completely helpless.'

You, O Lord, remain ever Yourself, abiding in eternity, good, just, and holy, ordering all things in goodness, justice, and holiness, and disposing them in wisdom. But I, who am always more ready to slip back than go forward, never remain the same, for seven times have passed over me. Yet, when You deign to stretch out Your hand to help me, my state is quickly changed for the better; for You alone, and without human aid, can help and strengthen me, so that I may no longer be unstable, but turn my heart to You alone, and be at peace. No mortal man can comfort me, and if only I could wholly renounce all human comfort – whether to increase my devotion, or because my needs compel me to seek You – then I could rightly trust entirely to Your grace, and rejoice in the gift of Your renewed comfort.

Whenever things go well with me, I offer thanks to You, from whom all proceeds. Before You, I am empty nothingness, a weak and unstable man. I have nothing of which to boast, nothing for which I merit any consideration. Can nothing boast of its nothingness? This would be the height of vanity! Empty conceit is like an evil disease, and the most monstrous of vanities, for it leads a man away from true glory, and robs him of heavenly grace. For so long as a man is filled with complacency, he displeases You; and while he hankers after popularity and praise, he is deprived of true virtue. True glory and holy joy are to be found in giving glory not to self, but to You; rejoicing not in one's own strength, but in Your Name; taking no pleasure in creatures, unless it be for Your sake. Praised be Your holy Name, not mine. I will praise your Name, but not my own; I will esteem Your doings, not my own: I will bless Your holy Name. I desire no share in the praises of men. You alone are my glory. You alone are the joy of my heart. I will offer You praise and glory every hour of the day; but for myself, I will glory in nothing, unless it be in my own weakness. Let the Jews seek such glory as men give to one another; I will seek the glory that God alone can give. For all human glory, all this world's honours, all earthly titles, compared with Your eternal glory, are mere vanity and foolishness. O blessed Trinity, my God, my Truth, my Mercy, to You alone let all things ascribe all praise, honour, power, and glory throughout endless ages.

CHAPTER 41
On Contempt for Worldly Honours

CHRIST. My son, do not be discouraged if you see others given honours and advancement, while you are overlooked and humiliated. Lift up your heart to Me in Heaven, and the contempt of men will not trouble you.

THE DISCIPLE. Lord, we are blind, and are easily deceived through vanity. If I carefully examine my life, I find that no creature has ever done me wrong, and I have no right to complain. But because I have so often and grievously sinned against You, every creature is rightly in arms against me. Shame and contempt are my just due; but to You, O Lord, be praise, honour, and glory. Unless I am ready, willing, and glad to be despised and abandoned by all creatures, and to be regarded as of no consequence, I cannot obtain inward peace and stability, nor can I become spiritually enlightened and fully united to You.

CHAPTER 42

That our Peace cannot Depend on Man

CHRIST. My son, if your peace depends on anyone, by reason of your affection or friendship with him, you will always be unsettled, and dependent on him. But if you turn to the living and eternal Truth, the departure or death of your friend will not distress you. Your love for a friend must rest in Me, and those who are dear to you in this life must be loved only for My sake. No good and lasting friendship can exist without Me, and unless I bless and unite all love it cannot be pure and true. You should be so mortified in your affection towards loved ones that, for your part, you would forego all human companionship. Man draws the nearer to God as he withdraws further from the consolations of this world. And the deeper he descends into himself and the lower he regards himself, the higher he ascends towards God.

He who attributes any goodness to himself,

obstructs the coming of God's grace, for the grace of the Holy Spirit always seeks a humble heart. If you would perfectly overcome self and set yourself free from love of creatures, I would come to you with all My grace. But while your interest is in creatures, the vision of the Creator is hidden from you. Learn, then, for love of the Creator, to overcome self in everything, and you shall come to the knowledge of God. But so long as anything, however small, occupies too much of your love and regard, it injures the soul and holds you back from attaining the highest Good.

CHAPTER 43

A Warning against Vain and Worldly Learning

CHRIST. My son, do not allow fair phrases and subtle sayings to beguile you; for the Kingdom of God comes not by words, but by My power. Pay attention to My words, for they fire the heart and lighten the understanding, foster contrition and bring all comfort. Never study in order to appear more wise and learned; study rather to overcome your besetting sins, for this will profit you more than will the grasp of intricate problems.

When you have read and mastered many subjects, always return to this fundamental truth: that I am He who teaches man knowledge, and who grants My children a clearer understanding than man can impart. He whom I teach will swiftly gain wisdom and advance far in the life of the spirit. But those who seek curious knowledge from men, and care nothing for My service, will discover only sorrow. In due time Christ will come, the Teacher of teachers and Lord of Angels. He will hear the lessons of all; that is, He will examine each man's conscience. He will search Jerusalem with lamps; the hidden things of darkness will be brought to light, and the tongues of controversy silenced.

I am God, who enable the humble-minded to understand more of the ways of the everlasting Truth in a single moment than ten years of study in the Schools. I teach in silence, without the clamour of controversy, without ambition for honours, without confusion of argument. I teach men to despise earthly things, to find this present life burdensome, to seek eternal things, to shun honours, to endure injuries, to place all trust in Me, to desire nothing but Myself, and to love Me ardently above all things.

There was once a man who loved Me very dearly, who learned My divine secrets, and spoke eloquently of Me. He profited more by renouncing everything than by studying subtleties. For to some I speak on everyday affairs; to others on particular matters; to some I graciously reveal Myself in signs and symbols, while to those who are enlightened I reveal My mysteries.

A book has but a single voice, but is not equally profitable to all who read it. I alone am the Teacher of truth, the Searcher of man's heart, the Discerner of his doings, and I give to each man as I judge right.

CHAPTER 44
On Avoiding Distractions

CHRIST. My son, you must needs be ignorant of many things: so consider yourself as dead, and crucified to the whole world. Furthermore, you must turn a deaf ear to many things, and consider only such as bring peace. It is better to turn away from controversial matters, and leave everyone to hold their own opinions, than to belabour them with quarrelsome arguments. So long as you remain in God's grace, and carry His Will in your heart, you will more easily endure apparent discomfiture.

THE DISCIPLE. Lord, to what a pass have we come? We grieve over a worldly loss; we labour and hustle to gain some small profit, forgetting the harm to our souls, and seldom recalling it. We attend to matters of little or no value, and neglect those of the greatest importance. For when a man devotes all his energies to material affairs, he rapidly becomes immersed in them, unless he quickly recovers his senses.

CHAPTER 45
How we should not Believe all we Hear

THE DISCIPLE. Lord, help me in my trouble, for vain is the help of man. How often have I found no loyalty where I expected to find it! And how often have I found it where I least expected! It is useless to place our hope in man; salvation is to be found in You alone, O God. In all that befalls us, we bless You, O Lord our God.

We are weak and unstable, changeable and easily deceived. None of us can guard himself so carefully and completely that he is never deceived nor in doubt. But whoever trusts in You, Lord, and seeks You with a pure heart, does not easily fall. And if he encounters any trouble, however great it be, You will swiftly deliver or comfort him; for You never abandon those who trust in You to the end. Rare indeed is a faithful friend, who stands by his friend in all trouble. And You, Lord, are the most faithful of all friends, and there is none like You.

How wise was the holy soul (Saint Agatha) who said, 'My mind is firmly established and grounded in Christ.' Were this true of myself, I should never fear any man, and no bitter words could disturb me. We cannot foresee the future or provide against evils to come; and if things that we expect often harm us, how can unexpected events do otherwise than seriously harm us? Why have I not made better provision for my unfortunate self, and why have I trusted so readily in others? For we are but mortal men, and nothing if not weak, even if many people imagine and say that we are angels. There is none in whom I can trust, Lord, save Yourself, who are the Truth, and who neither deceives nor can be deceived. But every man is deceitful, weak, unstable and fallible, especially in what he says, so that we should not at once believe even what at first appears to be true.

Your wisdom warns us to beware of man, since a man's enemies are those of his own household, and we may not believe any who says, 'He is here', or 'He is there'. I have learned this to my cost, and I only hope that it may make me more careful and correct my foolishness. 'Be discreet,' says one: 'Be discreet, and keep what I tell you to yourself.' And while I remain silent about it, imagining it to be a secret, he cannot himself keep the silence which he enjoined on me, but at once betrays both himself and me, and goes on his way. From such tales and from such indiscreet folk, protect me, O Lord! Do not let me fall into their power, nor behave in the same way myself. Make my conversation truthful and trustworthy, far removed from slyness. For what I do not tolerate in others, I must myself avoid at all costs.

To remain silent about others makes for peace and goodwill, neither believing all that is said, nor repeating what one has heard. There are few to whom we should open our hearts, but we should always seek You, who see into all hearts. We may not allow ourselves to be carried to and fro by the windy blast of words, but rather pray that all our life, both public and private, may be ordered in conformity to Your Will.

A sure way of retaining the grace of heaven is to disregard outward appearances, and diligently to cultivate such things as foster amendment of life and fervour of soul, rather than to cultivate those qualities that seem most popular.

Very many people have been harmed by publicity

and by lightly-bestowed praise of their virtues. But grace is most powerful when preserved in silence in this transitory life, which consists wholly of temptation and warfare.

[. . .]

CHAPTER 51

How when we Lack Strength for Higher Work we should Undertake Humble Tasks

CHRIST. My son, you cannot always burn with zeal for virtue, nor remain constantly in high contemplation; the weakness of sinful human nature will at times compel you to descend to lesser things, and bear with sorrow the burdens of this present life. So long as you wear this mortal body, you will be subject to weariness and sadness of heart. Therefore, in this life, you will often lament the burden of the body, which hinders your giving yourself wholly to the life of the spirit and to divine contemplation.

When this happens, you will be wise to resort to humble, exterior tasks, and to restore yourself by good works. Await My coming with unshakeable trust, and bear your exile and desolation of spirit with patience until I come again and set you free from all anxiety. Then you will forget all your former toil, and will enjoy inward peace. I will unfold before you the fair fields of the Scriptures, and you shall advance in the way of My commandments with heart at liberty. Then you shall say, 'The sufferings of this present time are

not worthy to be compared with the glory that shall
be revealed in us.'

[. . .]

CHAPTER 53
How God's Grace is not Granted to
the Worldly-Minded

CHRIST. My son, My grace is precious, and may not be
mingled with worldly concerns and pleasures. Therefore, if you wish to receive it, you must remove every
obstacle to grace. Seek out a place apart, and love the
solitary life. Do not engage in conversation with men,
but instead pour forth devout prayer to God, that you
may preserve a humble mind and a clean conscience.
Count the whole world as nothing, and place attend-
ance on God before all outward things. For you cannot
attend on Me, and at the same time take pleasure in
worldly things. Remain detached from acquaintances
and friends and independent of this world's consolations. It is for this reason that the blessed Apostle
Peter begs all the faithful in Christ to keep themselves
as strangers and pilgrims in this world.

With what confidence will a man meet death, to
whom no worldly affection clings! But a weak soul
cannot bear to be thus detached from all things, nor
can a worldly-minded man understand the freedom of
the spiritual man. Nevertheless, when a man sincerely
desires to be spiritual, he must renounce all, both

friend and stranger, and must beware of none more than himself. If you can win complete mastery over self, you will easily master all else. To triumph over self is the perfect victory. For whoever so controls himself that his passions are subject to his reason, and his reason wholly subject to Me, is master both of himself and of the world.

If you aspire to reach this height of perfection, you must make a brave beginning. Lay the axe to the roots, to cut out and destroy all inordinate and secret love of self, and of any personal and material advantage. From this vice of inordinate self-love spring nearly all those other failings that have to be completely overcome. But as soon as this evil is mastered and subdued, great peace and lasting tranquillity will follow. But few endeavour to die completely to self, and to rise wholly above it; consequently, they remain absorbed in themselves, and quite unable to rise in spirit above self. He who desires to walk with Me in true freedom must mortify all irregular and undisciplined desires, and have no selfish longing for any creature.

CHAPTER 54
On the Contrary Workings of Nature and Grace

CHRIST. My son, carefully observe the impulses of nature and grace, for these are opposed one to another, and work in so subtle a manner that even a spiritual, holy and enlightened man can hardly distinguish them. All men do in fact desire what is good, and in what they say and do pretend to some kind of goodness, so that many are deceived by their appearance of virtue.

Nature is crafty, and seduces many, snaring and deceiving them, and always works for her own ends. But Grace moves in simplicity, avoiding every appearance of evil. She makes no attempt to deceive, and does all things purely for love of God, in whom she rests as her final goal.

Nature is unwilling to be mortified, checked or overcome, obedient or willingly subject. Grace mortifies herself, resists sensuality, submits to control, seeks to be overcome. She does not aim at enjoying her own liberty, but loves to be under discipline; and does not wish to lord it over anyone. Rather does she desire to live, abide and exist always under God's rule, and for His sake she is ever ready to submit it to all men.

Nature works for her own interest, and estimates what profit she may derive from others. Grace does not consider what may be useful or convenient to herself, but only what may be to the good of many. Nature is eager to receive honour and reward: Grace faithfully ascribes all honour and glory to God. Nature fears shame and contempt: Grace is glad to suffer reproach for the Name of Jesus. Nature loves ease and rest for the body; Grace cannot be idle, but welcomes work cheerfully.

Nature loves to enjoy rare and beautiful things, and hates the cheap and clumsy. Grace takes pleasure in simple and humble things, neither despising the rough, nor refusing to wear the old and ragged. Nature pays regard to temporal affairs, takes pleasure in this world's wealth, grieves at any loss, and is angered by a slighting remark. But Grace pays attention to things eternal, and is not attached to the temporal. The loss of goods fails to move her, or hard words to anger her, for she lays up her treasure and joy in Heaven where none of it can be lost.

Nature is greedy, and grasps more readily than she gives, loving to retain things for her personal use. But Grace is kind and generous, shuns private interest, is contented with little, and esteems it more blest to give than to receive. Nature inclines a man towards creatures – to the body, to vanities, to restlessness. But Grace draws a man towards God and virtue. Renouncing creatures, she flees the world, loathes the lusts of the flesh, limits her wanderings, and shuns public appearances. Nature is eager to enjoy any outward comfort that will gratify the senses. Grace seeks comfort in God alone, and delights in the Sovereign Good above all visible things.

Nature does everything for her own gain and interest; she does nothing without fee, hoping either to obtain some equal or greater return for her services, or else praise and favour. But Grace seeks no worldly return, and asks for no reward, but God alone. She desires no more of the necessaries of life than will serve her to obtain the things of eternity.

Nature takes pleasure in a host of friends and relations; she boasts of noble rank and high birth;

makes herself agreeable to the powerful, flatters the rich, and acclaims those who are like herself. But Grace loves even her enemies, takes no pride in the number of her friends, and thinks little of high birth unless it be allied to the greater virtue. She favours the poor rather than the rich, and has more in common with the honourable than with the powerful. She takes pleasure in an honest man, not in a deceiver; she constantly encourages good men to labour earnestly for the better gifts, and by means of these virtues to become like the Son of God.

Nature is quick to complain of want and hardship; but Grace bears poverty with courage. Nature, struggling and striving on her own behalf, turns everything to her own interest: but Grace refers all things to God, from whom they come. She attributes no good to herself; she is not arrogant and presumptuous. She does not argue and exalt her own opinions before others, but submits all her powers of mind and perception to the eternal wisdom and judgement of God. Nature is curious to know secrets and to hear news; she loves to be seen in public, and to enjoy sensations. She desires recognition, and to do such things as win praise and admiration. But Grace does not care for news or novelties, because all these things spring from the age-old corruption of man, for there is nothing new or lasting in this world.

Grace therefore teaches us how the senses are to be disciplined and vain complacency avoided; how anything likely to excite praise and admiration should be humbly concealed; and how in all things and in all knowledge some useful fruit should be sought, together with the praise and honour of God. She wants no praise for herself or her doings, but desires that God may be blessed in His gifts, who out of pure love bestows all things.

Grace is a supernatural light, and the especial gift of God, the seal of His chosen and the pledge of salvation, which raises man from earthly things to love the heavenly, and from worldly makes him spiritual. The more, therefore, that Nature is controlled and overcome, the richer is the grace bestowed, while man is daily renewed by fresh visitations after the likeness of God.

CHAPTER 55
On the Corruption of Nature, and the Power of Grace

THE DISCIPLE. O Lord my God, You have created me in Your own image and likeness. Grant me this great grace, so necessary to my salvation, that I may conquer the base elements of my nature, that drag me down into sin and perdition. Within my being I can feel the power of sin contending against the rule of my mind, leading me away an obedient slave to all kinds of sensuality. I cannot resist its onslaughts, unless Your most holy grace is poured glowing into my heart to help me.

I need Your grace in fullest measure, to subdue that nature which always inclines to evil from my youth up. For it fell through Adam the first of men, and was tainted by sin, the penalty of that fault descending upon all mankind. Thus the nature which You created good and upright has now become the very symbol of corruption and weakness, for when left to itself, it leans always towards evil and base things. The little strength that remains is only like a small spark, buried beneath ashes. Yet this same natural reason, though hidden in profound darkness, still retains the power to know good and evil, and to discern truth and falsehood. But it is powerless to do what it knows to be good, neither does it enjoy the full light of truth, nor its former healthy affections.

Thus, O Lord my God, it comes about that, while I inwardly delight in Your law, and know Your commands to be good, just, and holy, both for the condemnation of all evil and the avoiding of sin, yet in my body I serve the law of sin, and obey my senses before my reason. Hence, while I indeed possess the will to good, I find myself powerless to follow it. In this way, I make many good resolutions, but, through lack of grace to support my weakness, any small obstacle causes discouragement and failure. Thus, too, I know the way of perfection, and see clearly enough what I ought to do; but I am borne down by the burden of my own corruption, and advance no nearer to perfection.

Lord, how urgently I need Your grace if I am to undertake, carry out and perfect any good work! Without it, I can achieve nothing; but in You and by the power of Your grace, all things are possible. O true and heavenly grace, without which our own merits are nothing, and our natural gifts of no account! Neither arts nor riches, beauty nor strength, genius nor eloquence have any value in Your eyes, Lord, unless allied to grace. For the gifts of nature are common to good men and bad alike, but grace or love are Your especial gift to those whom You choose, and those who are sealed with this are counted worthy of life everlasting. So excellent is this grace that neither the gift of prophecy, nor the working of miracles, nor any specula tion, however sublime, is of any value without it. Indeed, not even faith, or hope, or any other virtue is acceptable to You without love and grace.

O most blessed grace, that makes the poor in spirit rich in virtues, and the richly blessed humble in heart! Come, descend on me! Fill me with your comfort, lest my soul faint from weariness and dryness of mind. I pray, Lord, that I may find favour in Your sight, for Your grace is sufficient for me, even if I obtain none of those things that nature desires. However often I am tempted and troubled, I will fear no evil so long as Your grace remains with me.

Your grace is my strength, my counsel, and my help. It is more powerful than all my enemies, and wiser than all the wise. It is the teacher of truth, the instructor of doctrine, the light of the heart, the consoler of affliction. It banishes sorrow, drives away fear, fosters devotion, and moves to contrition. Without grace, I am nothing but a dry tree, a barren stock fit only for destruction. Therefore, O Lord, let Your grace always lead and follow me, and keep me ever intent on good works, through Your Son Jesus Christ. Amen.

[. . .]

CHAPTER 57
That we should never Despair

CHRIST. My son, patience and humility in adversity are more pleasing to Me than great devotion and comfort in times of ease. Why are you so distressed when you are criticized in some small matter? Had it been a far more serious matter, that is no reason for your being disturbed. Let it pass. It is not your first mistake, or anything new; nor, if you live long, will it be your last. You are brave enough when you meet no opposition. You can give good advice and encouragement to others, but when trouble knocks unexpectedly at your own door, your strength and judgement fail you. Remember the great weakness you often experience in small troubles; yet these things happen for your own good.

Banish discouragement from your heart as best you can, and if trouble comes, never let it depress or hinder you for long. At the least, bear it bravely if you cannot bear it cheerfully. Even if you are reluctant to bear it, and feel indignant, yet control yourself, and let no rash words escape you that may harm Christ's little ones. The violence of your feelings will soon subside, and grace return to heal your inner pain. 'I live,' says the Lord, 'ready to help and comfort you more than ever, if you will trust Me and call on Me with devotion.'

Be of good heart, and steel yourself to endure greater trials. All is not lost, however often you feel tempted or sorely troubled. You are a man, not God; you are human, not an angel. How can you expect to remain always in a constant state of virtue, when this was not possible even for an angel of Heaven, nor for the first man in the Garden? I am He who grants healing and comfort to those in distress, and I raise up to My Divinity those who acknowledge their weakness.

THE DISCIPLE. Lord, blessed are Your words! They are sweeter to my mouth than honey and the honeycomb. What would I do in such trials and troubles as mine, if You did not uphold me with Your holy words? So long as I come at last to the haven of salvation, what matters the kind or magnitude of my sufferings? Grant me a holy end, and a joyful passing out of this world. Remember me, O my God, and lead me in the right way to Your Kingdom.

CITY AND ISLINGTON
SIXTH FORM COLLEGE
283 - 309 GOSWELL ROAD
LONDON
EC1
TEL 020 7520 0652